A DOOR OPENS

A DOOR OPENS

Writing in Fifth Grade

■

JACK WILDE

Bernice A. Ray School
Hanover, New Hampshire

HEINEMANN
PORTSMOUTH, NH

HEINEMANN
A division of Reed Elsevier Inc.
361 Hanover Street   Portsmouth, NH 03801-3912
Offices and agents throughout the world

Every effort has been made to contact the copyright holders for permission to reprint borrowed material where necessary. We regret any oversights that may have occurred and would be happy to rectify them in future printings of this work.

The author and publisher would like to thank those who granted permission to use copyrighted material:

p. xii From *The Collected Poems of Octavio Paz, 1957–1987.* Reprinted by permission of New Directions Publishers, New York.

p. 109 "The Death of King Edward I," from *Medieval English Lyrics,* ed. by R. T. Davies. Copyright © 1964. Reprinted by permission of Northwestern University Press. Also reprinted by permission of Faber and Faber Ltd.

Chapter Two, "Fiction and Fact," first appeared in slightly different form as "Play, Power, and Plausibility: the Growth of Fiction Writers" by Jack Wilde. In *Breaking Ground: Teachers Relate Reading and Writing in the Elementary School,* ed. by Jane Hansen, Thomas Newkirk, and Donald Graves (Heinemann Educational Books, Inc., Portsmouth, NH, 1985).

Chapter Five, "Engaging and Informing," first appeared in slightly different form as "The Written Report: Old Wine in New Bottles" by Jack Wilde. In *Understanding Writing: Ways of Observing, Learning, and Teaching, K-8,* second edition, ed. by Thomas Newkirk and Nancie Atwell (Heinemann Educational Books, Inc., Portsmouth, NH, 1988, 1986).

Library of Congress Cataloging-in-Publication Data
Wilde, Jack.
    A door opens : writing in fifth grade / Jack Wilde.
      p.   cm.
    Includes bibliographical references (p.   ).
    ISBN 0-435-08761-4
    1. English language—Composition and exercises—Study and teaching (Elementary)—United States.   2. Fifth grade (Education)—United States.   I. Title.
LB1576.W4876 1993
372.6'23'044—dc20   92-30965
                                                                          CIP

Design by Debra Kam
Printed in the United States of America on acid free paper
01 00 99   DA   4 5 6 7

For Rachael and Jessica
My heart's strength

■

CONTENTS

■

ACKNOWLEDGMENTS

∎

I am not a writer. From childhood, I recall crumpled-up papers, the failed attempts to write letters to my sister. I remember the drawings I did for the cover of a report on chess, but not the report itself. I remember the struggle and frustration, the desire and the failure. I completed the term papers, the assigned reports and essays, but with an aversion to writing. I was not invested in it because I didn't feel I could make myself understood. I had no sense that I could alter the words, the printed thought on the page through revision or brainstorming; mine was one-draft writing. I can't remember celebrating a line of my own writing until my junior year in college when I had to find a topic for a paper on *Beowulf*. For weeks I wrestled with ideas—or rather, with a lack of ideas. With only ten days left, I found a subject that interested me. It seemed strong enough to support a paper. I didn't risk sharing the topic with the professor ahead of time. After eight weeks of going over the material, once I found a topic the paper almost wrote itself. Still, with no sense that that's how writing should always work, I felt no new confidence in my ability to write; I was only grateful that I had gotten lucky. In retrospect, I value that experience. It provides a signpost; I had the capacity to write. I did not, however, at that point understand the nature of writing.

I avoided writing as much as possible until I started pushing my students to write. They, in turn, exerted pressure on me. I resisted. But I also began to feel compelled to honor the commitment I was asking them to make. If they had to write, I had to write: trust for trust. I thank both my students at the Ray School and the participants in the New Hampshire Writing Program. Their insistence lies behind this book.

The encouragement to write for publication came from Tom Newkirk. He not only prodded me to write what I had spoken, but supported me from inception to publication. I am indebted to him for his constant encouragement. Through his many invitations I have uncovered my writing voice and dared to use it.

Tom also included me in my first community of writers by asking me to teach in the New Hampshire Writing Program. This book reflects the insights and reactions of many of my fellow instructors: Jane Kearns, Tom Romano, Terri Moher, Linda Rief, Susan Stires, Paula Flemming, and Ellen Blackburn Karelitz. I also appreciate the close reading of an earlier draft of this manuscript by fellow classroom teacher David Millstone. At Heinemann, my editor, Philippa Stratton, has been a model of patience and forbearance as the book's scope changed and deadlines passed.

Throughout, from my early faltering attempts to the final manuscript of this book, I have had one first editor: Mary Ann. She struggled with me to fashion a text. This book is the better for her efforts to get me to say what I mean with whatever grace I am able.

With all this help, support, and encouragement, I have written. As an emerging writer I continue to struggle to write effectively—to make my prose fluid, my ideas concrete. The errors and missteps are mine. I realize now, in ways I had not accepted, that they are part of what it means to be a writer.

INTRODUCTION

∎

I have been an elementary classroom teacher for twenty-one years, the last ten as the language arts teacher in a departmentalized fifth grade. For those same ten years I have also been an instructor in the New Hampshire Summer Writing Program. The combined experiences have forced me to explain, justify, and reshape my classroom practices. My repeated explanations, and fellow teachers' expressions of interest, prompted me to write this book.

Initially I intended to write only about my classroom teaching: what I do and why, illustrated by student work. I have done that. Chapters two to six present the ways I teach personal narrative, fiction, poetry, persuasion, and informational writing. Each chapter looks at a genre or writing task, suggests ways that I invite and encourage both drafting and revising, and offers student work to demonstrate the kind of response I receive. With these chapters, I do not offer a recipe for teaching. Rather, in the process of presenting practice, I raise issues for teachers to think about in introducing and supporting writing: issues like modeling, topic restriction, and genre experience.

But the book is about more than that. As I wrote, I found myself becoming more visible, even prominent, in what I had written. I had intended to show only my work and thinking; I ended up revealing much more of myself. Why? Narcissism? An inability to explain? No—or, at least, I don't think so. Rather, I wanted to say something about attitude and experience in teaching. Using the teaching of writing as a specific example, I wanted to make a more general point about the evolutionary nature of teaching: that it is an evolutionary process with historical determinants. Teaching, I believe, is an art. Like all artists, teachers go through various stages, each a combination of personal history, reflected experience, and a deliberate intention (however ill-informed) to create. In any artistic endeavor there must be a number of false starts, missed opportunities, outright mistakes, inspiration from unsuspected sources, and general muddling that only becomes clear in retrospect. I have tried to capture all these aspects of teaching: first, by documenting my own history; second, by explaining the assignments as they exist in my classroom now, and showing how they developed; and third, by showing ways in which my general experience informs my thinking about teaching and learning.

Octavio Paz, the Mexican poet, writes about poetry as "an act/ an act of speech." I see this book as a deed. By its very existence it proclaims the teacher's right and need to go beyond the classroom, to present oneself and one's work. Too often we in the teaching profession are told what to do and how to do it. We are told to paint by the numbers and call it art. Administrators, textbook writers, and college theoreticians tell us how to do our jobs. No give and take; no colloquy; only direction. And too often we allow tests, workbooks, or designed curricula to control our teaching. Each teacher-written piece presented by publishers like Heinemann or in journals such as NCTE's *Language Arts* helps enfranchise teachers. Each claims the teacher's right to develop curriculum—goals and means. This right, like all rights, entails responsibility. We must hold ourselves accountable for the learning in our classrooms. But this right, when realized, allows us to draw on all of our experience to inform our teaching. I make no claim to having better ideas than others, or to having found the one right way. Rather, I claim the right to present and discuss ideas about teaching.

All three layers of intention—myself as emerging teacher, my classroom practice, and my desire to reach beyond my classroom—are present in this book: not developed as independent strands but interwoven. I invite you to read the following pages and see what one teacher has done with writing.

· 1 ·

Learning Teaching, Teaching Learning

My faculty adviser turned toward me, surrendering his gaze on the New York City skyline. "You've made a good choice to go into teaching. Let the City pay for your master's, then go on and get a doctorate, and end up teaching two days a week and living in Dutchess County."

I looked at my hands; I couldn't look at him. Only a year out of college, I had enthusiastically enrolled in this program, not to take the City for a free master's, but to teach in Harlem. Still too inexperienced to challenge authority directly, I feigned understanding and acceptance, signed the necessary papers, and left, forgetting Dutchess County in the sweltering June heat that met me at the professor's door. Neither his comments nor six weeks of summer school in un-air-conditioned quonset huts diminished my desire to teach. The course work almost did. As an undergraduate I had majored in history, with no thought of going into teaching. These were my first education courses. It felt like junior high school shop class. We learned to identify educational objectives, to write lesson plans, and to expect the worst. We practiced our lessons on each other, finding our only relief from the heat and tedium in acting out future students' misconduct on the unwitting practitioner of the day.

Starting to Teach

Upon completion of the summer work, I was assigned as an above-quota teacher to P.S. 175. The assignment confirmed the worst: I would spend the year as a permanent substitute. But on the last workshop day before school was to begin, I was reassigned to a first grade. First grade! All my mental preparation that summer had been for a fifth- or sixth-grade class. What did first graders need? What would I do? I spent that Friday preparing my room, trying to make the cinder-block cubicle that would house twenty-five six-year-olds and myself inviting. I came back on Saturday with pictures and burlap to dress the room up even more. As I decorated the room I wondered: What were my objectives for these children? To help them learn to read and do math. That was all I could come up with.

I don't recall the specific plans that I had for my first day. Whatever I thought I would do collapsed as I opened my classroom door. The room had been ransacked. All the pictures, maps, and posters were gone. The room looked the way it had before I had begun work on it the previous Friday. Somehow I got through the day with games, discussion, and a little work.

Much of the year felt the same. Rather than acting on my beliefs about teaching, rather than planning how to achieve my objectives, I reacted to situations: I felt the control lay outside myself. My objective, such as it was, became simply to get through the year and have the students learn—no easy task with school lockouts, withheld paychecks, and third-grade extortion rings that forced my first graders to pay to walk down the hall without being beaten up. Yet counterbalancing the bad were some moments of exhilaration: walking down Broadway on a snowy December day with all the students spontaneously breaking into song; seeing the excitement on their faces when we saw a whale in the Museum of Natural History; feeling pride at their general level of accomplishment on the citywide reading test.

That year I did have my students do some writing. Workbooks and dittos were everyday fare. They were the "real" work, as recognized by the school. But occasionally we would use large ruled paper to write one- or two-sentence journal entries or to create a story. Twenty minutes for this. There was nothing in the environment to encourage me to do more. My own inexperience with writing confirmed the school's avoidance. My sense of effectiveness as a teacher came from test results, not from my students' creations.

The year I spent teaching in Harlem had been time away from coursework at Union Theological Seminary. I had taken the teaching internship with no intention of continuing to teach. I saw the year as an opportunity to serve. But back at Union I became restless, wanting to *do,* tired of being a student. After another year at Union, I was offered a teaching job at a private school, and I took it. There I had a supportive administration, an abundance of materials, and time to plan. I could not simply react; I had to become involved. With little formal training in education, I let the environment dictate an area of interest. In a cupboard I found some wonderful old math workbooks published by Encyclopaedia Britannica. They were different from any math material I had seen. Instead of telling the student to carry out an arithmetic operation and presenting a number of examples, this book turned the assignment on its head. Students had to try to determine, through various partially completed examples, what they were to do on the page. There were almost no directions. Some called for arithmetic computation—for example:

1	2	3	4	6	__
12	24	36	__	__	72

$$1 \rightarrow 3$$
$$2 \rightarrow 7$$
$$3 \rightarrow 11$$
$$6 \rightarrow \underline{}$$
$$\underline{} \rightarrow 31$$

Others did not:

O X V O O O X V O __ __ __

At first my five- and six-year-olds resisted this approach. They wanted to be told what to do. But gradually they derived a begrudging satisfaction from figuring out what was going on.

Within a month the students and I were beginning to feel comfortable with this different approach to teaching and learning math. I realize in retrospect that I often asked them to do things that were too abstract, and that I controlled the experience more than necessary. Yet, even with those drawbacks, both they and I were excited by the learning and teaching.

The next year, working with seven- and eight-year-olds, I continued to experiment, now making up my own material and starting to use Martin Gardner's games in *Scientific American*. During those two years I discovered that teaching is learning, finding out what works and doesn't work and how much others can learn. I ended the year having the children write problems or stories about unknowns. One boy was a Beatles fan. He wrote, "Paul McCartney made one less than twice as many records as Ringo Starr. Together they made twenty-nine records. How many did each one make?"

That year I was twice blessed, because not only did my students help me discover the excitement of math, but I also got to meet and discuss math education with one of the authors of the Encyclopaedia Britannica material, Walter W. Sawyer. By fortunate circumstance I knew Professor Sawyer's daughter. Once I became aware of his work with children, I imposed on the friendship with his daughter: I got an invitation to a conference in Toronto where Professor Sawyer was presenting a workshop to a group of elementary teachers. He explained his belief: Children need to develop an understanding that the basis of mathematics is the search for patterns, patterns that are not immediately obvious. Computation is only a small subset of the world of math, but in elementary school we tend to define math as computation. Even more excited and convinced after my discussions with Mr. Sawyer, I went back to my classroom committed to having my students experience real math, not textbook arithmetic.

Two years later, after completing a year each in two different private schools, I moved from New York City to Hanover, New Hampshire. Not a city boy, I couldn't imagine raising a family without grass and private space. From 1972 to 1980 I taught first grade and then third grade. In those years I solidified my commitment to discovery or inductive teaching in math and began to extend it to science, helping students hypothesize about causes and remedies for erosion. And unwittingly I used the inductive approach in other areas of teaching as well.

Teaching Writing

During my first ten years of teaching, I did not ignore writing. Although math drew much of my attention, writing was a classroom activity from the beginning. Most of the writing consisted of whole pieces or journals. Not knowing what I should or shouldn't expect of them, I had my first graders keep a journal for the second half of the year. They wrote in them every day, after the noon recess. I monitored them and provided spellings. As someone who wrote only when necessary, I had no personal writing skills or experience to call on. And in the six-week summer-school session I'd attended in New York City the word "writing" wasn't mentioned once. Handwriting, yes; writing, no. Left to my own devices, I thought of journals. The second year I added poetry to journal writing. I began to have students memorize poems and then write poetry. I can no longer recall the specific trigger I used to get students to write "feelings" poems, but I still have their work. (Who says teachers are pack rats?) Max wrote:

> Butterflies fly
> Be free
> But it's a matter I can't
> Fly. In this poem it ex-
> plains my free feeling.

The next year we wrote poems again, and I added Kipling's "Just So" stories. I read several of Kipling's tales to the chidren, and we discussed how he composed them. We identified the tools he used: explanation of a natural phenomenon, humor, repetition, and big words (used correctly or incorrectly). Then my students wrote their own. They explained how the leopard got its spots, the deer its antlers, the pig its curly tail. I remember Nicky's story:

> HOW MAN LEARNED TO TALK
> Once a long, long time ago there was a monkish personish and there were vegetables and the person hated artichokes and once he ate an artichoke and said, "Yuck, disgusting! Blech!" And that's how people learned to talk.

I liked the results I got with the "Just So" stories, and I continued to have students write them when I moved from first to third grade. I expected my third graders to do even more writing. Colleagues used story starters; I used other models of writing. I had my students read *Hailstones and Halibut Bones* (O'Neill 1961) and we wrote our own color poems. We studied Japan in social studies, so we read and wrote haiku. In 1976, after teaching third grade for three years, I introduced a new writing unit— mysteries. An admirer of William Pene DuBois, I read *The Three Policemen, The Horse in the Camel Suit,* and *The Alligator Case* with my class. I realized that they understood the genre and could write their own mysteries. As with the "Just So" stories, we discussed the elements of the genre: a crime, clues, a detective, a criminal, suspects, plot development. We spent time shaping the personalities and habits of our characters, came up with a plot line, and wrote. Some students had difficulty sustaining their mystery, often making the criminal an easy catch. But the stories worked. Indeed, many of them worked quite well. Here is a section of Steve's mystery about a stolen Picasso painting:

One night at about 10:15 the 5 foot 8 inch, 16 year old detective Peter Fleetz enters his office in Los Angeles. He has fine straight blonde hair that glitters in the faint light. You can tell that he is happy when his bright blue eyes light up. His nose sticks out from the rest of his face with a few freckles. His red lips brighten up his whole face. He wears a plaid shirt five days of the week and black shoes that go with it.

An hour later when Peter was about to fall asleep, the phone rang. Peter jumped out of bed surprised by the noise. He picked up the phone. It was the Metropolitan Museum of Art curator. He started in a panicky voice.

"At 11:00, when we were changing guards in the painting section, someone killed the changing guards by a knife that was laying on the floor just a minute ago, all bloody. But the worst part was he stole Picasso's painting The Three Musicians and got away. Nobody saw him.

"We all know that you are the best detective in the country, and mostly in paintings. Could you come and help solve the case?

"Mr. Reeds, the head guard, is calling your brother to come help," said the curator calming down.

"Okay, I'll be there at 6:30 a.m. Bye, see you in the morning."

After some trying adventures Peter did get his man, who turned out to be the curator!

Learning

If this account conveys little thought on my part about the writing assignments, it captures my actual level of involvement during those years. Though not uninterested, and though willing to look for new writing experiences, I did not give them a lot of thought—certainly not as much as I was giving my math work. I liked the results of the assignments, but I left it at that.

My approach and thinking about writing began to change in the summer of 1979, when I participated in the Bay Area Writing Program in Exeter, New Hampshire. It took an act of naive hubris for me to apply. I still had not written outside of school, nor had I read a single article or book on the teaching of writing. I did not know what to expect. That was probably fortunate. Had I thought more about it, I might not have risked starting down the writing path. In the program, each of the participants had to make a presentation to the group. I was first. I presented my mystery unit to thirty teachers of kindergarten through college. Afterward, a high school teacher said; "Your kids are dealing with the same issues as my seniors." That was news to me; already I was learning just from presenting.

The four weeks proved long but revealing and exciting. Don Graves, Don Murray, and Tom Newkirk all came from the University of New Hampshire to make presentations. I learned that people were thinking about approaches to writing. Much was said about James Moffett; I read his *Student-centered Language Arts K–12* (1992). I wrote on my own for the first time. In particular, I struggled to write a poem: the first poem I had ever attempted.

Back in school that fall, I didn't change my practice much. My third graders continued to write journals, "Just So" stories, poems, and mysteries. But I did start to think about my teaching interests. I made a commitment to focus on language arts in my upcoming sabbatical year, and to return to Hanover to teach language arts in a departmentalized fifth grade.

In 1980 I was granted a sabbatical to study at the Ontario Institute for Studies in Education. I went expecting to further my newfound interest in language arts. I went there specifically to study with Frank Smith. He left that year. As a result I did work in psycholinguistics, focusing on Piaget. I felt ignorant in educational psychology. I certainly knew Piaget's name; I'd even heard him speak once. But I didn't understand his stage theory of cognitive development. In the course of reading his work I was drawn to his ideas about mathematical operations and numbers. I had come to OISE to work on reading and writing, and I was back doing math! But the draw of Piaget was not that his concepts confirmed and illuminated my experience; rather, my experience challenged his idea of invariant stage development. My professor encouraged me to do some original research to examine some of Piaget's positions. I chose the concept of number conservation.

Piaget believed that children must have a correct spatial sense of numeracy before they can add or subtract with understanding. "Correct spatial sense" means that they are not distracted by how long a line of beans is, but can focus on the number of beans in the line, regardless of how they are spaced. My research suggested that children need not pass through this step before being able to add or subtract with understanding. They could, but it was not a necessary cognitive step. I felt vindicated, convinced that I had not been forcing premature abstractions on my students, but was tapping capacities many students possessed.

While I did some work on math, most of my courses addressed issues in reading, writing, and language development. I found myself reacting to much of what I read in the theory of writing development the same way that I had reacted to Piaget. I shouldn't have been surprised, because much of the theory was based on a Piagetian model. Both Moffett and Andrew Wilkinson, an English researcher, were explaining through assignment and assessment what children at various ages could and could not do. Each, in his own way, held that young children can only write egocentrically—that is, they are unable to imagine the needs of a reader other than themselves; they are unable to write in formal ways that call for de-centering (for example, essays, editorials, critical analysis). Moffett and Wilkinson's research suggested that students were essentially bound to write this way until around age thirteen, when "formal operational" thinking allowed them to write abstractly. I was simultaneously attracted and repelled. I was attracted because the theory was logical and compact. In their model the mind is like a flower. In the fullness of time the mind becomes fully formed and able to take on all tasks. While forming, the mind has potential, but not the ability; it is only a bud, not a smaller flower. But I was also repelled because, as with Piaget, the theory denied my experience with children. My students had written mysteries and "Just So" stories that were not egocentric pieces. But most important, all my third graders had written, and written a lot.

The previous year, I had had a Down's syndrome boy who was mainstreamed. Steven could not read, so I decided that I could not ask him to write. He decided otherwise! He wanted to be part of my class, to do what the rest of us were doing. We had to come up with a way to make it work; he was insistent that it work. Finally we found that he could dictate two or three sentences. We would write them down and leave a space below each line so that he could copy each word. If, within a reasonably short space of time, he were then asked to share the sentences, he could get the gist, often the thought in its entirety. Steven taught me how strong the desire to write can be. I must never exclude students from writing. Moffett and Wilkinson did not seem to be describing the world of students I knew.

I came back from my sabbatical to my new teaching position ready to focus on writing. The first two years I tried to think through not only the models of Moffett and Wilkinson, but also the emerging model of teaching writing in elementary school that Don Graves captured with crystalline preciseness in *Writing: Teachers and Children at Work* (1983). Tom Newkirk, then an assistant professor at UNH, sealed my involvement by inviting me to become an instructor in the New Hampshire Writing Program for the summer of 1981. The invitation and my acceptance made me reflect on my classroom practice. Explaining to other teachers what I did, and why, meant that I needed to understand my teaching practices in a new way. Specifically, I had to be clear about my teaching with regard to the proposed practices of Moffett, Murray, and Graves.

Understanding Teaching

If the first part of this chapter sheds any light on who I am as a teacher, then my conclusions about my relationship to these people's work should come as no surprise. My theories of teaching come out of my lived experience. I am not Don Graves, James Moffett, or Don Murray. Teaching is not a glove that one slips on to perform in the style of another. We willingly acknowledge that in an artist. A painter, sculptor, or writer works from experience, experience that includes theory, reflection, and the interaction with the work of others. We are less likely to acknowledge experience as an important factor in a teacher. I carry with me all the teachers who have taught me, and all my teaching experiences: camp, day care, Sunday school, Harlem, the Upper East Side, and Hanover. My experience is filtered through an exposure to the teaching and thinking of others. It is also subject to my own reflection. But my theories of teaching can never be disconnected from my experience. I cannot teach like Don Graves. One size does not fit all. Rather, we must shape our teaching to conform to what we know to be important in teaching, and to what we know of ourselves. Writing is like hitting a baseball; we acknowledge the important principles, but we must each find our own way to capitalize on our strengths. Stan Musial, Ted Williams, Mickey Mantle, Duke Snider, and Willie Mays were all effective hitters. Each found his effectiveness in a different stance, one that captured his own experience and knowledge. Teaching is a stance toward learning.

Graves's and Murray's works are expressions of what they believe, know, and practice. It is their turn at the plate. I cannot ignore their work either as a rookie or as a seasoned veteran. As a language arts teacher I must know what others think and do in my profession. But I also must not feel that I am called to become them. Often that pressure is hard to resist. In the early 1980s I was concerned because my students were not revising as much as Graves said they should. Because they weren't, I felt that I wasn't teaching writing. A story that my cousin tells about herself illustrates the way that I was thinking. Lynn, a nurse just out of nursing school, began work in an intensive care unit. She had been instructed that should the line on a patient's oscilliscope become stationary, that meant cardiac arrest, and she must immediately administer a sharp blow to the chest, to shock the heart back into beating. One day, as Lynn visited with an elderly patient, she looked up at the oscilliscope, saw the stationary line, jumped on the patient's bed and started thumping on his chest. Caught in mid-sentence by her first blow, the man managed to cry out, "What are you doing!" Lynn had let training override experience. Her instruction had momentarily prevented her from considering that the oscilliscope might have malfunctioned or become disconnected.

I made the same mistake, not judging the overall experience I was providing for my students, but only the lack that Graves's book helped me see. I took autobiography for prescription. In this book I am not writing prescriptively. Nor do I now think that Graves, Moffett, Wilkinson, or even Piaget were. They were all working out what they believed in the light of their experience. All models and theory should be seen as interactive. They allow us to think together about common issues and concerns. It is with this intention that I present in the succeeding chapters what I do in teaching writing: not as prescription, but story. It is the story of a teacher trying to find effective ways to teach.

My adviser was right when he said I made a good choice in going into teaching. Teaching is fascinating, exhilarating, depressing, confusing, complex—alive. Hearts and minds intersect to share and explore our world. We need to explore the discipline as we need to write: not in isolation, but together. Here are my ideas and practices worked out in my fifth-grade classroom.

· 2 ·

Fiction and Fact

My fifth-grade students have a strong sense of story. They should. For years they have been read to, watched movies and TV shows, and played a variety of video games; each of these media has a strong narrative cast. Many of my students have been asked to create stories at home or in school. Their minds and senses have imbibed story. Creating stories is comfortable and safe. No surprise then that these students, when given the opportunity to choose a genre and write, choose stories: fictional stories. In creating their pieces a familiar pattern recurs, a pattern drawn from experience: the stories are controlled by adventure. Like video games, "Miami Vice," choose your own adventure stories, and "Indiana Jones and the Prophet of Doom," adventure drives the story—*is* the story. While humor is often present, sometimes description, occasionally telling detail, they all serve the action. Here is an excerpt from Chris's story "War with King Kong" that illustrates a ten-year-old's approach to fiction writing:

> Ten minutes later, when Mark and Patrick got to school in their tanks and planes, they saw King Kong. Mark started firing his machine guns. Two of the bombers started bombing. Most of the tanks started firing their guns.

King Kong was just about to step on the school when Mr.
Vogel ran up to him and yelled, "Don't step on my school!"

So instead of stepping on the school, King Kong stepped on
Mr. Vogel.

Chris's writing is playful power. He creates a world that fulfills
his wish (the human wish) for control. He answers the fiction
writer's question "What if?" applied to himself: "What if I were
all-powerful?" In his created world he rewards himself and his
friends while demolishing all enemies, including Mr. Vogel, the
principal.

Writing Facts

Stories like Chris's created a problem for me. As a teacher
I wanted to help students become better writers, to help them
improve their skills. These stories resist improvement. The
constant refrain "That's the way I want it to work in my world"
defeats efforts to get them to expand, alter, or re-focus their
stories. They expect the action—chases, fights, feats of physical daring—to carry the story, not the writing. Like so many
B movies, the assumption is that violence and suspense are interesting in and of themselves, especially when personalized. Simply
present fighting and the story works. And many peer reactions
confirm such an idea. Adventure does sell. But it doesn't improve
writing or give the writer a more complete sense of what writing
entails. I worried about my students' sense of craft, while they
celebrated their easy victories.

Previously, with the "Just So" stories and mysteries, I had
simply chosen a genre that the students could understand and use
as a model. I hadn't given much thought to what they were
learning about the craft and conventions of writing. Now, more
aware of the writing process, I began to think about ways to help
students experience elements of the process, specifically revision.
I found Don Graves's argument for personal-experience writing
persuasive. My students resisted revising their stories. When
a point was raised about something in their stories that did not
make sense, they would simply reply that that was the way their
made-up world worked. Writing out of personal experience
could provide an important corrective to such an attitude. The

writing could be compared to the experience it was based on. If the two were not congruent, the writer would work (revise) to make them so. Writing about experience, I thought, could provide an impetus to revise and a way to look at revision. Convinced of this, I had my students write about themselves. Many of the children resisted: "Nothing exciting ever happens to me; there's nothing to write about." Their fertile imaginations dried up. Those who did find a topic wrote about trips or accidents; something exciting had happened to them. They let the weight of the event carry the story. Rather than crafting a story, they reported an event.

Instead of becoming better writers, they regressed, fumbling in their attempts to present an experience. But the problem was not theirs; it was mine. I had provided no models of memoir writing. I had assumed that they could extrapolate from fiction to memoir. Both genres are narrative, but they are decidedly different. The writer can and does create in both, but not in the same way. Students had little experience reading or writing memoirs. I needed to provide that experience through modeling and discussion. Models show possibilities and establish a general level of expectation. Now I read parts from Roald Dahl's *Boy,* and Annie Dillard's *An American Childhood.* I also share pieces written by fifth graders from prior years. Now I encounter less resistance from my students, and their writing seems better.

REVISION

Even in the first years of writing personal experience stories, when drafting was not supported by modeling, students were more open to revision. In conferences we talked about what worked well and why, and then raised questions about those parts of their stories that were unclear, confusing, or inadequately developed. The students accepted the need to revise. Most of their changes were minor, substituting a different word or adding a sentence or two. Still, most improved the papers. Writers made the stories easier for readers to follow and become involved in. Here are two examples. In the first, Bonnie writes about her house being struck by lightning. She worked hard to make clear the condition of the house after the lightning had struck it. She revised to make her ending more effective. Printed below are Bonnie's first and final drafts. Read them for their overall effectiveness. Look for ways that she worked to make the final draft stronger. Note specifically her inclusion of details in the final version and her use of comparisons at two important points in the story.

Here is Bonnie's first draft:

It was about 6:30 P.M. The rain came down like cats and dogs. There were immense flashes of lightning and the sound of the raging thunder was very alarming. My Mom was making dinner in the kitchen and me and my sisters were in our family room playing games. We were all very frightened of the lightning then. Just a little while after my sisters and I had been playing games, the storm became very strong. All of a sudden there was a giant flash of lightning and a huge bang of thunder. We heard a shriek from my Mom. So we all ran into the kitchen and there was my Mom on the floor and nails were half out of the dented ceiling. A lamp had popped from the ceiling and there was broken glass all over. As my Mom got up she told us how she saw a big flash of lightning come toward her and how it crashed on the house and destroyed the whole kitchen.

When we had finally all settled down, my Mom called my Dad at work. When my Mom told him what had happened he said he would be home in approximatey fifteen minutes. In about an hour my Dad got home and he talked with my Mom and said they would call some people in the morning.

And her final draft:

It was a cold autumn evening. The time was about 6:45 P.M. The rain came down like cats and dogs. There were immense flashes of lightning and the sound of the raging thunder was very, very alarming. The lightning had put me, my mom and my sisters in complete darkness, because of the power failure. Even though it was quite dark we were able to find flashlights and get candles to burn.

My two sisters and I were in our family room playing games. I was really whipping my sister Anna in the game "Chicken Out!" My mom was in the kitchen making a salad which we had voted on earlier that day.

All of a sudden we heard the rain tumble much harder and the wind blow much stronger. Just as a giant bolt of lightning came down, my sisters and I heard a scream from the kitchen. We ran into the kitchen and there was our mom on the floor with terror in her eyes. I ran over to her and gave her a hug. Then she hugged all of us.

When mom finally settled down and got up, she told us that a big flash of lightning came towards her and before she knew what had happened it had hit the house. When I looked at the kitchen, the lamp from the ceiling had popped out and there was glass all over the floor from the kitchen windows that had broken. There was a big dent in the roof of the kitchen and nails had dropped out of the ceiling.

I was very scared of everything that was happening. I was only five years old and I thought the house had died.

My mom took my little sister and me by the hands and put us in the livingroom. My older sister Anna followed. Later we all got together on the couch and my mom tried to explain to us that it would be all right. After about six minutes, my mom got hold of a telephone and called my dad at work to tell him what had happened. He was shocked! He said he would be home in fifteen minutes. It turned out to be forty-five minutes.

When he finally got home he said he was sorry he was late but he got an important phone call and he couldn't hang up. When he saw the kitchen he was quickly on the telephone getting someone to come and start fixing up the kitchen.

The earliest someone could come was 11:30 in the morning. So he said that was fine. The guy came at 11:30 the next morning and said he could start right away. So he did. Day after day, month after month, the guy came with his men. Finally in about two or three months the house was finished, and I was very happy! I felt like a flower being watered after many weeks of dryness.

In the next example we see a student willing to choose a seemingly unexciting event and craft it into a story. Annie worked not only on topic choice, but also on description. She wrote about a day she and her dad spent riding bikes and enjoying the countryside. After a lengthy ride, which included a race, they stopped to rest in a field.

"Can I climb the willow tree?" I asked.

"Sure, go ahead." So I started to climb the tree and soon I found a place where the bending branches were shaped like a chair. I got myself settled and looked around. "Wow," I said. It was so beautiful with curtains of green sunlight. I peeked through cracks in the leaves. My eyes started to close and I was about to fall asleep when a little summer breeze came up and the light branches swayed.

I almost fell out of the tree. "Yikes," I grabbed a branch and held on until I got my balance back. The next time a breeze came up I was fine as the branches swayed softly. I got down from the tree in a few minutes.

My dad was asleep so I decided to take a walk. But instead of walking I crawled, looking at things that live in the tall grass. I was crawling along and I put my right hand down. Something wrapped around it. I gasped and looked down. "Whew," I said. To my relief it was only a Garter snake. I picked up the snake; it unwrapped and dropped off my hand. It was really fast in getting away. It was nice to see that it was so fast so that the snake could get away from danger.

Just then I heard my dad calling, "Annie, Annie where are you?"

I stood up: "Dad, I'm right here."

"Oh, hi. It's about time we leave, so let's go." I was kind of sad to leave the field, but I knew we would come back.

We went home and I was right about going to Storrs Pond because we went right there and Jenny, Mary Pat and Katy were there, too.

The next year we went back to the field. Neither the willow tree nor the field had changed a bit that I could see and I was glad of that! I went to the willow tree, climbed it and found the place in the tree where the chair was. It felt like the same day as last year. I hadn't changed a bit either.

In conference we talked about the ending. Originally the story ended with Annie joining her friends at Storrs Pond. Was that a strong ending? Did it leave the reader with the feeling she wanted the reader to have? Chronologically it might have been the next event and brought closure to the bicycle trip, but did it bring closure to the trip as a story? Annie went back and worked some more on the ending. She remembered that she had gone back the following year; she had more information that might serve as an ending. So she pulled the reader out of the immediate chronology of events and moved to the next year. In so doing she, like Annie Dillard in *An American Childhood,* reflected on her experience. An effective way to end a reminiscence.

Still other students listened to the models and then found their own ways of presenting their experience. Andy wanted to write about his trip to Disney World but did not want to give a blow-by-blow account of the trip. He turned his piece into a description and a rating of the different rides. For example:

> The first ride I went on was Mr. Toad's Wild Ride. Ride Rate: 8 (a Ride Rate is a rating of the ride from one to ten). The next ride we went on was 20,000 Leagues Under the Sea. Ride Rate: 9.5 (I'd give it a ten but its line was too long).
>
> Chapter 3: The Ending
> It would take all year to explain the rest of the day, so I'm editing it to two sentences. The Jungle Cruise R.R. 9 (so I like to abbreviate, sue me!), The Pirates of the Carribean R.R. 9.5.

Andy avoided the "and then we did . . ." piece. He created a fresh approach to present the rides and the most important information: how good each ride was. He offers partial justification for this move in his ending by suggesting it would take too long to explain all the rides. While we might want to know more about his criteria for judging and his actual experience on the rides, Andy's classmates liked his story. His approach engendered interest. They liked the way he drew on general knowledge—the use of rating scales for evaluating movies, Nintendo games, and some sporting events—and applied it to his vacation. They also liked his brash voice: "So I like to abbreviate, sue me!" The students liked the way Andy confronted the reader. His story, like the others, is a series of choices—of style, content, focus. Each piece reflects the student's voice, the interaction between the writer and the response group, and the conferences with me.

The stories do much more than tell the experiences interestingly. They also present the students' accompanying internal states—their reactions, thoughts, and feelings. My earlier writing assignments lacked this component. The "Just So" stories and mysteries used other conventions to generate and sustain reader involvement—a branching story line with false clues in the mysteries, and a loose causal connection in the "Just So" stories. Neither needed a psychological aspect. Personal-experience stories do. Nor was I alone in wanting to know the writer's feelings and thoughts. In conferences, peers wanted to know what the author felt while living through the experience. How did Bonnie feel when the house was hit by lightning? How did Annie feel about her day? Which rides did Andy like best?

Together we began to set more writing goals. A new writing experience, writing autobiographical stories to foster revision, became an opportunity to look at product as well as process. Techniques of prewriting and revising, specifically multiple drafting of leads and conscious revision through deletion, addition, and moving text, provided the chance to explore process, and at the same time pushed us to write more complex pieces—to write better stories, stories with some psychological depth.

In so doing we began to move beyond one of the problems of children's writing—cuteness. Too often, in all areas of endeavor, children are encouraged to settle for cute instead of striving for good. Cute may have a place, but it must not supplant honesty. Children feel the press of popular culture everywhere—TV, music, greeting cards, computer games, movies. And almost everywhere that culture simplifies experience. Cuteness doesn't honor the world's complexity. It doesn't stretch the creator or the audience. It has a self-satisfied air that freezes rather than frees.

Whether the psychological aspects were presented or not, part of the goal in the students' writing became to write more knowingly about themselves and the world. In each of the stories discussed earlier there is a quality of reflection, not simply a retelling. That quality is there in Bonnie's comparisons—"I felt like a flower being watered after many weeks of dryness." Andy's reflection comes through in the comparative ratings of the rides. Annie creates a sense of reflection in her ending. She must have changed in the year since she last sat in the tree. So she stretches the truth—stretches toward cuteness—in saying that nothing had changed. At the same time, her last paragraph, written only when she was pushed to do so, reflects the desire we all have for things not to change. Did she know that when she wrote those sentences? I doubt it. But she can grow into her words' meanings. Right now her sense of connection, of going back to re-see experience, is enough. The process of writing, sharing, and revising has her extending an experience, thinking past it to something more. That something more got her to remember returning to the tree a second time and feeling the same way—a more complex reality, stacking experience on experience. This added complexity I hadn't anticipated when we started to see where writing about experience would take us.

TOPIC CHOICE

While I found new ways to encourage my students to grow by incorporating Graves's suggestions, I also found points of resistance. Topic choice was one. I began teaching writing by assigning genres and limiting topics. I found that a difficult stance to abandon. I still haven't, but Graves pushed me to think more clearly about my position. Basically, I felt, and still feel, that restriction can enhance opportunity, and not always limit it. Topic choice in its most extreme form is topic freedom. And that kind of freedom can create paralysis. Not knowing where to turn, how to judge, or even what constitutes an option, the writer freezes, often falling back on some structure when none has been provided.

Further, topic choice in its extreme form misrepresents writers' experiences. Few writers feel that they have topic choice in the sense of having complete freedom to write about whatever they want to write about. Most writers acknowledge that they are bound by experience and circumstance. The artist Ben Shahn presents an excellent explanation of this condition in his book *The Shaping of Content* (1957). As an artist working for a newspaper in Chicago, he was assigned to cover a fire. He sketched the fire and produced a picture for the newspaper. But he could not leave the experience there. He continued to work with those images. Finally he produced a new print called *Allegory*. It brought together his thoughts and images of fire. The topic developed because of the assignment, not in spite of it. Work often gets done because of the exigencies of existence, not in the freedom of a heavenly garden. Topic choice to me means making a topic one's own, finding a way to invest in a topic. That's what Ben Shahn did, and that's what my students do. I must leave them room to invest. That's why I don't require them to write about the scariest thing or the funniest thing that's happened to them. But I will ask them to write about themselves, because they can learn something about revision, about another genre, about another way of using written language to explore and explain the world.

Fiction Holding Fact

Personal-experience writing was not intended to supplant fiction in my classroom. It didn't. Students continued to want to create whole stories. I wanted to honor that desire, at the same time focusing on revision and helping them broaden their sense of the scope of fiction. I found an answer to both concerns in the books we were reading: Norton Juster's *The Phantom Tollbooth,* Theodore Taylor's *The Cay,* Lloyd Alexander's *The Book of Three,* Katherine Paterson's *The Great Gilly Hopkins,* and Frances Burnett's *The Secret Garden.* All are adventure stories, but with an important difference. In each, a character goes through a change of personality in the course of the story; adventure is not an end in itself. It represents experience. Each story presents the dynamic interplay between character and events. In most student fiction, characters shape and control events—the power is in their hands; in these stories, characters do shape some events but are also shaped by them. The death of Mary's parents in *The Secret Garden* forces her to interact with people very differently than the way she did with her indulgent parents. The torpedoed boat and Phillip's subsequent blindness in *The Cay* forces him to interact with someone he never would have otherwise. In the process, Phillip changes, matures. He is not simply floating through a world that he can control, pulling out an Uzi or jumping into a jet when the going gets too tough. The dynamic is controlled by a psychological reality that is reenforced by the plausibility of character and circumstance. The circumstance can be far-fetched, as it is in *The Phantom Tollbooth* with Milo and the watchdog Tock traveling to imaginary lands, but the effect of the experience is real enough. Milo learns the compelling force of journeying, of seeking something, and loses his sense of ennui in the process. We, the readers, accept this because that is the nature of a quest; psychologically it rings true.

The stories require three elements in addition to plausibility in order to work. The reader must know:

- The character's personality at the outset.
- The event or events that alter the character's personality.
- The character's changed personality.

THE ASSIGNMENT

Having established the necessary ingredients of a good story through discussion of some of the books we've read, I begin the assignment proper by reading my students a short story by Ivan Turgenev, "The Quail." It is the story of a boy who wants more than anything to hunt with a gun like his father; a boy who, in the end, because of a specific incident, will never hunt. When I finish reading the story I ask the students how the character has changed and how they know this. Then I ask them how they think they have changed or people around them have changed. We then make lists, individually and collectively, of observed and possible changes in people. At this point I am always asked if change can occur only in one direction, from characteristics that are less desirable to those more desirable. The question is answered through discussion, as students acknowledge that changes can be in a negative direction.

Next, we decide if the event in "The Quail" seemed plausible to us: Would it result in the stated change? We start making lists of plausible reasons for change. I push them to make long lists (i.e., ten reasons) so they will stretch themselves and, in so doing, discover ideas and feelings they didn't even know they had. We talk about the reasons for change together, testing them for plausibility, trying to decide if we need one reason or several for the projected change.

At the same time we talk about and work on character description. We look back at the stories we've read to see the different ways that characters are made known to the reader—through dialogue, anecdote, and action. We learn much about Phillip in *The Cay,* for instance, through his discussions with Timothy. We read specific passages that show character traits, then try our hand at writing dialogue to reveal character. After trying several different approaches to character portrayal, the students choose one and begin their stories.

There is a strong push in this assignment toward revision, because a story only works if the character is drawn convincingly and the events can be accepted as bringing about the stated change. Conferences, then, focus on character description, action, and plausibility. In full class meetings, in small group conferences, and in student-teacher conferences we ask:

- Do I get a clear picture of what this character is like?
- Does my sense of the character match the author's intention?
- Do the actions of the characters fit their personalities?
- How does the character change?
- Are the events in the story sufficient to cause the change?

The assignment—to write a change-of-character story in which the main character goes through an internal change—addresses the concern I had about process in fiction writing. Not only is there a clear litmus test to measure whether a draft needs revision or not, but also the nature of the genre requires some planning and collecting of thoughts before drafting can begin. There must be some order for the piece to work; the character cannot change by magic.

THE RESULTS

As one would imagine, the results vary widely. Very few children have difficulty understanding the assignment. Almost all of them can identify character change and the elements of character change in the stories they read. But there is a difference between understanding and doing. Of those who end up not writing about a change at all, most are too wedded to a real character or a real situation and are unable to fictionalize the story. One girl, for instance, tried to change her best friend from a constant classroom clown to a contrite, committed student. She had the girl get into trouble and prepare to change, but, in the end, the author wrote that she could not change. There were other students who achieved partial success. Daniel is one such student.

Daniel had difficulty writing personal narrative. He would do anything to avoid journal writing or personal storytelling, but he had a keen sense of humor and a willingness to write in any other mode. For this assignment Daniel created a character, Bill Porkorn, who came into a lot of money selling pork. He used the money self-indulgently to go to Hawaii. He then came into some more money when the rest of the pork sold. Bill's reaction was to think of all he could buy—a yacht, a big limo, a swimming pool. At this point Daniel originally had Bill's friend, Joe, pick up a newspaper. Joe reads Bill a story about the famine in India. Bill immediately decides to give money to Oxfam.

When Daniel met with his peers for a group conference, they asked about the sudden change in Bill's character. For them, there was no event sufficient to warrant the change. Daniel, with some peer advice, went back and worked on his story. He made the information about the famine reach Bill through television news, feeling that would have more impact. Then at the end of the story Daniel added:

> Joe was on Bill's back until Bill donated the money. The large donation was announced on TV. Bill was interviewed many times. Because of this, Bill made many more donations, large and small!!!

Almost as an afterthought, not discussed specifically in the peer conference, Daniel included a realistic psychological component to Bill's gift-giving. The initial event is not sufficient to warrant the action, but the self-serving tag of notoriety confirms Bill's former character while helping the reader see that he could change his attitude toward spending money. There was no psychological reality in the original transformation. Now there is some. Plausibility came into play as Daniel revised the story; otherwise he would have simply changed the medium from newspaper to television. Here revision serves to make the story work.

Julie spent hours planning her story. Little was written down. She wrestled with her ideas in her head. She had decided that her character, Mr. Whitestaff, an elderly loner, would go from being outwardly mean and gruff to being welcoming and accepting. She knew that the pivotal event would be the presentation of a kitten to Mr. Whitestaff by Clara, an eleven-year-old who would initially have a chance encounter with him. This much decided, Julie worried whether such a change could occur with just this single event. She decided that that was not plausible. Julie expressed her concern this way in the conference: "How should I get to the end? I know what's going to happen in the story but I don't want to get there too fast." I looked at her. Before I could speak, Julie went on, as she usually did: "He couldn't change that fast. I know! The girl could come several times, maybe with flowers." Fortunately I hadn't spoken. Many of the most productive conferences work this way: in talking past the listener to oneself, one solves a problem. Julie did little revising because she did so much planning; this is another approach to generating successful pieces. Here is Julie's story:

One brisk June morning I woke up feeling very radiant. I jumped out of bed with tremendous energy. Summer vacation had just started. I put on my new birthday outfit, brushed and braided my long red hair and finally skipped out of my room. When I entered the kitchen, I saw my Mom. She was in her blue plush robe reading the paper. "Hi Mom," I said.

"Hi Clara," she replied. "What do you want for breakfast?"

"Shredded Wheat but I'll get it." I reached up in the cabinet to get a bowl then to the cabinet to the left to get the Shredded Wheat. I settled down and began eating when all of a sudden the phone rang.

"I'll get it," my Mom screamed. I continued eating. She talked for awhile and then hung up.

"Claaara" she called. "Be a doll and go over to Archibald Whitestaff's and get a package of ours that accidentally came to his house."

"Oh, I don't want to. I hear he's very mean."

"Now, Honey, you'll only be face to face with him a minute."

"Ohhh," I replied.

"Thanks, Hun."

I walked out the door feeling nervous. What if he yells at me? I thought. I walked up a path that leads to a small meadow filled with Goldenrod, Paintbrush, Dandelion, and scentful Clover. Its beauty made me feel confident. I wished I could stay there and dream forever. I lazily walked through the meadow. Finally I came upon a bank. A rabbit lolloped into the distance. I followed a path through some brush and then finally came upon a big old

Victorian house surrounded by rose bushes. I went up the walk and knocked on the door. It was a long time before I heard some puttering about in the house. Finally, the big oak door opened. I felt small and scared as I looked at the tall slim figure dressed in a red velvet robe.

"Yes," he said in a very gruff voice.

"I-I I'm here" I said looking into his sad grey eyes, "to get the package that came here by accident."

"Just a minute," he replied and walked back in the house grumbling. I waited a minute until he came back carrying a small box.

"Here," he said handing the box to me.

"Thank you," I said in a small, tight voice. I turned and got half-way down the lawn when Mr. Whitestaff yelled at me.

"Hey you there. Were you the child who broke a twig off my $12.00 rose bush?"

"N-No Sir. I've never been to your house," I said. "Goodbye." I started across the lawn again when he yelled, "I know who you are—you're the one who knocked the petals off a tulip of mine."

"No Sir, I told you. I've never been to your house before. I'm sorry, I really have to go." I made it to the very edge of the lawn when he yelled, "You're one of those juvenile delinquents who smashed my grass down, aren't you?" This time I didn't even bother to go back. I just yelled, "No, I'm not. I just have to go now or my Mom will worry."

As I walked through the meadow I thought "Dumb ole insane man—I hope aphids eat all his $12.00 rose bushes." I ran all the way home. As I ran into the mud room Mom said, "Whoa! Slow down! What's the matter?"

"Well, nothing really—Um (pause) Why do you think an old man would ask me if I broke a twig off his rose bush and little things like that? He knew I've never been by his house."

"Well, he's old and he lost the one person left in his life and now he's very lonely. Maybe he wanted you to stay but he did not know how to ask you."

"Oh, I see," I said, feeling a little better. "I wish there was something I could do. I mean it's kind of sad."

"Honey, there is something you can do. Be his friend. Talk to him. Let him work his way into your heart," said Mom gently.

"But how?" I questioned.

"Just talk to him."

"OK, I will tomorrow."

The next morning I woke up, pushed away my down comforter, and got out of bed. I put my hair in a pony braid, put on a pretty but plain print dress, and went downstairs. I went into the kitchen and fixed my usual Shredded Wheat. While I was eating my Mom walked in. I quickly finished my last bite and said, "Mom, I would feel weird going to Mr. Whitestaff's for no reason. It's like Hi Mr. Whitestaff. I'm here to let you into my heart." (ha ha)

"Well you mentioned he said something about smashing his buttercup. Get a pot, plant one, and give it to him."

"Oh, that's what I'll do, thanks."

"Yep," she replied.

I walked to the mud room and got a summer coat, then to the greenhouse. I combed through the pile of junk and found a nice pot. I walked out into our tulip patch and dug up a bulb with a nice flower. I got some gardening soil and potted the bulb. I went in and told my Mom where I was going and left. I walked through that pretty meadow and then up the bank. The large house came into sight. I walked up the steps and knocked. In a few seconds that old oak door opened. I got that same feeling, that same small scared feeling as the velvet robed figure appeared.

"Oh, it's you again. Come here to finish off my $12.00 rose bush?"

"Eh? No, I came—well—to give you this" I said, handing him the pot. "It's a—well—a repayment since you think I crushed the petals of a tulip. So here's a tulip."

"Oh great, another something to water, but thanks anyway."

"Yep," I said.

I was just about to turn and leave as he said, "Oh, by the way, you can come to tea. Probably you juveniles would rather play video games than have tea with an old man so I won't be expecting you. I have tea at 10 A.M."

"Bye," I said. "I'll ask my Mom." I walked home feeling good. Well, I thought. I'm making him less mean. I walked into the house and told my Mom what had happened. She was very pleased.

"Do you think I should go?" I asked.

"Of course, Honey and take it seriously."

"Oh, Mom."

That night I slept with content.

The next day I woke up, put on a dainty party dress, put my hair in plaits, and did other morning basics. I ate breakfast and was ready to go.

"Mom, I'm going," I yelled. I walked towards Mr. Whitestaff's being careful not to dirty my dress. I arrived at his house one minute late. He answered the door. Instead of his usual red velvet robe, he was wearing a baggy pair of old man pants, a blue shirt, and a safari jacket.

"You're a minute late but come in anyway," he said.

He led me into a boring formally decorated room. It was furnished with a small couch with a lace cover, an oak drop leaf table, old vases, a marble top table, a dusty oriental rug, and finally a huge bookcase featuring Mark Twain, Charles Dickens, etc., etc.

"This way" he mumbled as he walked into a dining room. As I followed him I felt sorry for him. I tried to imagine him eating all alone at the huge long table three times a day. On a tray by the table was some tea and cookies.

"Sit down here," he said, pointing to a chair.

We both sat down and he passed some tea and cookies. As I was eating I asked him some questions. When was his birthday? How long had he lived here? etc., etc. That seemed to push a button because he started talking, blurting out personal stuff like about his wife dying.

At the last of my cookie I looked at the clock and said, "I better go now."

"Oh, sure," he said a little disappointed. He led me to the door and opened it.

"Goodbye" he said.

"Yep, goodbye and thanks. I had a good time," I said meaning what I said.

During the next few weeks I went to his house a couple of times. Each time he was a teeny tiny bit less gruff and sad. For instance, the first few times I saw him he greeted me with an almost cheerful grin. Still, he had a lot to change.

One night I was awakened by an awful crying type of noise. I walked around the house but it stopped. I was still interested in what it was so I went to the guestroom and looked.

There was my cat, Tabitha, with a litter of newborn kittens.

About seven weeks later, we had given away three kittens. We still had one really cute one left. Anyway, one morning I was eating breakfast and I had a really good idea.

"Mom," I said. "Didn't I tell you Mr. Whitestaff's birthday was July 20th?"

"Yes, Honey, I believe you did."

"Oh good. That's tomorrow. I think I'll give him Tabitha's last kitten."

"Oh, Honey, that's a very good idea." That night I went to bed feeling good.

The next day I got ready and ate breakfast. I got the kitten, put a bow around its neck, and left. I knocked on Mr. Archibald R. Whitestaff's door. He answered,

"Oh, hi. What brings you here, Clara?"

"Happy Birthday" I said as I gave him the kitten.

"Oh thank you," he said as he gave me a hug. "Thank you for everything."

I knew I had a very special friend.

Julie did the assignment more effectively than I imagined possible. She provided the reader with a believable character and turned him loose on the page to reveal himself to us. She was conscious of the need for plausibility. She shows through her story that change, especially change of this magnitude, is often gradual. We see this in the gradual change in Mr. Whitestaff's attire and greeting. Julie added the correct psychological touch by having Mr. Whitestaff acknowledge his gratitude at the end not in words, but by a hug.

Fact To Fiction

Another option is working from fact to fiction. The idea for this was triggered by my work with Katherine Paterson, specifically discussions of her book *Bridge to Terabithia*. In that book Paterson fictionalized the experience of her son David to better present the friendship between a boy and a girl and the boy's coping with the girl's death. In talking about the book she quoted Kipling: "Fiction is truth's older sister." We can tell some things with more psychological accuracy by fictionalizing than by trying to recount the actual experience. Fictionalizing can be as small a move as changing the name of the real person, or as large as changing the gender or age or setting.

Sarah was in many respects an angry child. Before writing the story below she had written several personal-experience stories in which people had let her down. She stayed focused on her experience. Sarah used the fictional story as an opportunity to explore the character of someone other than herself; she chose her brother. She changed her brother's name so she could better present him. Changing his name freed her to present her brother. With a change of name she could now enter the character's mind, plumb that psychological awareness, and let the character carry out actions consistent with his inner state. Not bound by having to represent actual occurrences, Sarah could explore what it might be like to be her brother.

"Paul, clean your pony's stall."

"Right now," he whined.

"Yes, right now!" she snapped.

He groaned. He knew he had to do it, but the work he had to do to keep the pony as his own, he despised. And the sun burned hard which made him sleepy and grumpy. Paul turned toward the barn, his mother went back to pulling weeds from the garden.

When Paul reached the barn he (with difficulty) pulled on the huge sliding door. With a groan the door gave in, and slid open to the left. Paul opened the stall door and went to get a pitchfork. After cleaning the stall he went out to the chicken coop to cheer himself up. As he rubbed his sweaty back, he patted Peep-Peep, the pet chicken.

"Good girl," he crooned as he stroked her chin. Peep-Peep made some sounds in her throat to indicate to him to keep petting her.

Paul then left off suddenly and ran into the barn. He closed his pony's stall door. As he entered the tack room he turned to the feed bin. He opened the bin and took out a handful of horse grain.

When he got into the chicken coop he hand fed the grain to Peep-Peep. After feeding the grain to Peep-Peep, he glanced at his mother. She had her back to him. With a smile he ran over to the fence, climbed over and jumped out. Now safely in the sheep pen he relaxed. He slowly strode towards the sheep who were grazing near the shed, picking dandelions and pulling off their heads to his great delight.

When he reached the sheep they raised their heads to greet him. The identical twin lambs raised their heads to look him over. He patted the sheep for a while but finding them boring he retired to the house. When he entered the house he was greeted by his mother, who was standing on the front steps with her hands on her hips.

"Clean your room right now!"

He rolled his eyes and snorted. It was true, he had not really cleaned up his room. He plodded upstairs groaning. He turned right into his room. He pushed the guinea pig cage back against the door. Then, kicking the wall as he went, he walked over to his desk. After watering his plant, and putting things in order and making his bed, he went outside again.

"Paul, lunch!" his mother screamed.

"Coming!" He blindly shouted back, counting on. Suddenly he wheeled around and ran towards the house.

"Here, let's eat outside," said his mother, handing him a sandwich, two carrot sticks, and a cup of lemonade. Paul and his mother sat down on the terrace chairs eating lunch peacefully when . . .

"Mom, this stupid sandwich keeps falling apart."

"Are you holding it with both hands?"

"Well, no-o."

"You should know at the age of seven how to keep your sandwich together!"

With that Paul lost his temper. He tossed the rest of his lunch (half a sandwich) to the dog, who caught it in mid-air. Paul went up to his room to feel sorry for himself.

Trent presents an extrapolated emotional state. He wrote this story as he prepared to move from Hanover, the only place he had ever lived.

Winslow Innes stared from his big bay window at the stormy ocean in front of him, reflecting on his twenty years running the lighthouse he called home.

He had received a letter from Washington earlier that day telling him they were going to automate his lighthouse. It was the only manually operated one left on the coast of Maine.

Trent then has Winslow remember why he had come to the lighthouse and recall many of the pleasant moments he had spent there. His reverie is broken by a knock at the door.

Thud! Thud! Thud! A noise echoed through the lighthouse. Winslow opened his eyes. "I must have been daydreaming," he said to himself. He walked to the front door. A small man in a pin-striped suit said nervously, "Mr. Winslow Innes?"

"Yes, I am he."

"Mr. Innes, the time has come to leave the lighthouse. I judge by the look on your face you got the letter."

"Yes, I did."

"Then can you pack your belongings and be out by tomorrow?"

"Yes, I can."

"Well, I will see you tomorrow."

That night Winslow could not sleep. He decided to take one last walk around the island. He put on his jeans and a turtleneck and walked sadly around the island. The island seemed smaller than ever so he walked slowly. As he crossed the meadow the lighthouse loomed in the distance. He walked up to the door, put the key in the lock for the last time, and walked quietly up the spiraling stairs.

The next morning he packed up his personal belongings and put them in his dory. For the last time he made the trip across the bay but as he came close to shore he turned and started paddling out to sea until all that was left of him was a dot on the vast horizon.

The Fiction Assignment Now

Just as the thrust of mathematics is the search for patterns, the thrust of most modern fiction is the psychology of relationships. I want my students aware of both. But awareness and performance are two different things. When I played "What's My Rule" in first grade, I didn't require that everyone participate in the game. But I wanted everyone aware. So we would sit in a circle, and I would let those who could figure out the rules provide answers and explain their reasoning to those who had difficulty. I now do the same with the psychological component of writing. We look at examples, and those who see the operative principles identify and discuss them. As a whole class we think about change-of-character stories and stories that present fictionalized events. But then I let individual students choose how they will approach fiction. For some, a single discussed example of a story in which a character changes is enough to whet their appetites and help them develop the confidence to write such a story. Others need more exposure. Some may never try. All can write either realistic or imagistic fiction. The choice is theirs. It's a choice informed by all their past reading and writing, and our present reading and discussion. They are all learning that math is more than adding, and fiction can be more than power and entertainment: it can be a place to explore psychological reality.

All of these approaches are not to deny the importance of play and imagination in fiction. My purpose is not to belittle the uses that my students have made of writing and fiction, but to extend their options, helping them to realize all that can be done in writing. Many ten-year-olds can recognize psychological motivations in the actions of others and themselves. Most can recognize those motivations in the stories they read, and some can begin to incorporate that awareness into their writing, whether it be fact, fiction, or a hybrid. I am constantly learning what students can do by what they do do. I am convinced that many of them can write with some psychological depth. I can help students discover that ability in themselves, increasing their awareness of ways they can better know themselves and the world.

· 3 ·
Uncovering Poetry

I cannot call up a detailed image of Miss Sawicki, my eighth-grade English teacher, just a presence—a large physical presence cloaked in drab print. I do remember, however, that she introduced me to poetry. I'm sure that basals in earlier grades included poetry: ornamental notes to writing's major theme—stories. I had read *The Merchant of Venice* in seventh grade, but as drama, not poetry. Miss Sawicki brought poetry closer to center stage, but her choices and personal presence were countervailing forces to the presence, the force, that poetry can command. As a teenager I saw only the utility of language; any celebration of the power of language occurred in scatological locker room remarks. Miss Sawicki confirmed my apathy toward poetry. Her favorite poet, Joyce Kilmer, could inspire little in me—a tree is a tree. This confirmed my ennui for classroom life that was only occasionally broken by conspiratorial snickerings at her sentimentality. This was my formal introduction to the study of poetry.

Subsequent high school and college English courses attenuated my poetic encounters, turning most poems into conundrums to be solved, puzzled out. Always the teacher knew, knew unerringly, what the poem meant. And I didn't. Except for a college course on Dante's *Divine Comedy,* I can't recall a time when the study of poetry involved extensive reading of the poetry aloud. It was presentation without the poem being present. I was never asked to write poetry, only dissect it, unravel the poet's message and intention. My apathy was reconfirmed. I can only remember buying one book of poems in those years. It was a collection of poems by the British poet Philip Larkin. That purchase was stirred by reading an anti-religious poem of his in *The Nation,* a chance encounter. Moved by the subject, I bought the book. But poetry had no place in my life.

Teaching Out Of Ignorance

I actively avoided poetry until I started to teach. Even then, I was not drawn to it for several years. My first use of poetry with younger children had them memorizing short poems for choral readings. As a virtual stranger to poetry, that was all I felt competent to do. I wanted oral language to be part of my students' education and felt poetry would work best. This was in the late Sixties, before the whole language concept and much of Bill Martin's work. I ventured into poetry alone. I did ask students to write poems about their feelings (like Max's in chapter one), but they were given no model and I had no clear goal except for the writing to sound "poetic." Two years later, with six- and seven-year-olds, I gave my first formal poetry writing assignments. I'm not sure why. With my tin ear and lack of rhythm, developed by years of disuse, I resorted to the wholesale use of models to drive the assignment.

Mary O'Neil's *Hailstones and Halibut Bones* served as the model for color poems. We figured out as a class the categories she addressed and then did the same: "Red is the color of. . . ." I felt ill at ease with the process and the product, but didn't know why.

Myra Cohn Livingston's book, *Child as Poet: Myth or Reality?* (1984) has helped me, in retrospect, to understand the disquiet. Her book challenges the idea that formulaic poetry is poetry in process or product. Further, she questions the use of formulaic poetry as a teaching tool to be used with the young. Specifically she calls into question the techniques and assignments used by Kenneth Koch. She argues that his teaching methods have several drawbacks. First, his method creates instant poetry—an impossibility for a poet. With his plug-in lines ("I used to be . . . but now . . ."), the students simply fill in the blanks, accumulating lines and calling the result a poem. Livingston concludes that one can get a good line from such an exercise, even a good idea, but not a poem. Second, the line and the poem are unlikely to be grounded in experience, real or psychological. The lines often encourage an outrageousness that knows no bounds. It neither accepts experience nor plays off of it. To represent such work as poetry is to sell the work, the experience, and the product short: to call painting by the numbers art.

My assignment in many ways mirrored Koch's: the formulaic line, little responsibility to reality, and the hurry to finish: one-draft poems. I know that now; I didn't know it then. The disquiet festered until I started to learn about the writing process—until I began to write. I attempted my first poem as an adult with nine years of teaching experience. I had been requiring my students to write poetry for six years. Only in the act of writing poetry myself did I start to discover why I might want to pack words so tightly, to walk closer to the inexpressible. But even then I didn't know how to translate that knowledge and experience into classroom practice. My students continued to write color poems and haiku.

Rethinking Poetry

Only when I started a writing process classroom could I see that my poetry work had to change, and how that change could take place. I wasn't willing to give up on poetry, despite my personal discomfort. What to do? As with the students' other writing, I decided to draw more directly on their experience of poetry and of life. The change started not by doing something new but by using what we did differently. I continued to have my students memorize poetry and present it orally. But now those poems would become the foundation for our definition of poetry, a functional definition to help us start to sense what makes poetry poetry. Before, I had simply assumed a poetic definition that was implicit in the color poems or haiku. In so doing we as a class had never discussed the how and why of poetry. We had simply followed the formula given by me or derived by the class—for example, the number of syllables, the change of feeling, the subject matter in haiku. Now we would take a broader sweep, looking at all the poems we'd memorized. I made sure that my choice of poems was even more eclectic, in order to broaden the students' sense of what poetry can be. Among others, my students now memorize poems by cummings, Frost, Dickinson, McCord, Ciardi, Hughes, and Kushkin. First I select specific poems; then they choose from a limited number of anthologies. I avoid Shel Silverstein, not because his work isn't poetry, but because if my students read any poetry on their own, they read his. I don't need to encourage or support his poetry; I need to expand their experience. The memorization and presentation of poetry is just the first step. Those encounters form the reservoir of experience that we will explore.

After memorizing eight to ten poems and reading dozens more, we begin to discuss what makes a poem a poem. Usually for homework I ask students to record their favorite lines of poetry, to try to state why they find those lines effective, and then to write down what makes a poem poetry. The first part of the exercise gets the students to think about the poems they have read and learned. The functional definition grows out of the discussion of our written thoughts. There is no right answer. I am not looking for a dictionary definition but a sensibility that we can take into our writing. Here is a list of characteristics of poetry that one class came up with:

- short version of a story
- choppy
- rhyme (not have to)
- rhythm
- lines/stanzas
- more description
- flow
- looks differently on the page
- shorter
- not always makes sense
- adjectives
- repetition
- aloud
- comparisons
- words put together differently
- sing-song
- about nature—good things/not always
- feelings
- doesn't have to tell a story

As we think about the what and why of poetry, I ask the group to talk about several contradictions in the list. Is poetry only about good things? Must a poem be narrative or nonnarrative? Does a poem have to rhyme? Why do poems ever rhyme? What is important is that the definition is student generated for student use. They begin to look at the techniques of poetry—the tools—and not the specific meaning. The poem is. In the phrase of the Mexican poet Octavio Paz, poetry presents, not represents. We are looking at how poetry presents itself—not as one formula, one poetic style or form as I did before, but in general how words can become a poem. As the list above demonstrates, the definition encompasses sound, sight, and language meaning. The discussion is designed to put the children on the inside exploring how to mean and be in language; they are on a continuum with practicing poets. Only in the dictionary is there a static definition of poetry. For writers the definition must be dynamic: the tension between meaning and being, intent and content, feeling and knowing, saying and not saying.

While I have freed my students from a specific form or a tightly controlled model, I haven't freed them completely. I've learned (as other chapters suggest) that I can often heighten the writing experience by exercising control over the assignment's topic. Concerned from my years of having them write "Red is . . ." I want to shape the experience so they can get a legitimate sense of the power poetry may hold for them. In the process I hope also to authenticate their experience. My decision (and I don't mean to suggest that it is the only decision or necessarily the best) is to ground the writing directly in experience. While we're discussing the idea of poetry in general, I continue to read to them, to offer them examples. I read several poems from *Reflections on the Gift of a Watermelon Pickle* (Dunning, Lueders, Smith, comp.). As before, we talk about what works, what seems effective in the poems, questions we have for the author, other reflections. After reading the children "Base Stealer," "Foul Shot," and "Child on Top of the Greenhouse," I make an additional point: each one of these three poems deals with a few brief moments in time, moments felt intensely. Of course that is not the only subject of poetry, but it is one. And it is one that we can use to connect poetry to experience, while getting away from straight narrative. We feel the pull of words to match emotional intensity. This approach addresses Livingston's concern that writing come out of a felt need to express something, that it not be generated by a gimmick. H. L. Rosenthal in *The Poet's Art* (1987) speaks about the felt need as the lyric center of poetry. The poet Donald Hall (1988) has written that twentieth-century poetry deals with the intensity of feeling. So our schoolwork has the students deal with a central issue in modern poetry. And it puts writing experience in the correct order from felt need to words, rather than the reverse. Koch believes that the formula will generate poems, not simply serve the poetry muse. In the very outrageousness of "I used to be a grape, but now I am wine" the writer may strike a truth. And that may happen; gimmicks do have their place. But for most of us as beginning writers the kind of associationism Koch offers makes poetry a kind of mental gymnastics divorced from a need to speak or be heard. Most of us need to find that felt need and then see where the connections will take us. So, yes, there can be play, but within the need to say something.

Children's poetry needs to be grounded in a way that connects language with experience, forcing both the writer and the reader to reconsider experience. The assignment is shaped to foster such a connection. It can't ensure the outcome, only push in that direction.

From Prose To Poetry

The next step in the process requires students to come up with a brief, fleeting experience intensely felt. Robert Francis's poem "The Base Stealer" doesn't describe how the base stealer got on base or what happened to him that inning, but just the moment of electric tension as the runner dances off first base. It's not a story; it's the feelings of the moment. The assignment helps focus on the feelings as opposed to the story. The students must do the same: find a moment, a charged moment. And then, through the poem, communicate that moment to the reader.

My students work on this by trying to recall all the sensory data of the moment. By category they recall the information: sights, sounds, tastes, smells, touches, and thoughts. With that information as a base and the functional definition as a shaping influence, they begin to write, to shape the experience, to make it accessible to another. Jenny, a fifth grader, decided to write about the first time she went off the high dive. She had been asked to recall twenty-five pieces of sensory information and the feelings connected with the experience. Jenny came up with the following:

Touch
hands pushing in my side
hair dripping on my feet
eyes closed
toes moving
windy
water cold
water got in my nose
legs together

Tastes
sour

Sights
eyes closed
water shining

Sounds
silent after
splash
people shouting at me telling me to go faster, and to hurry up

Smells
flower

Inner feelings
scared
I blinked to look down
I stepped forward
stomach spinning
feet hit the water
splash
felt wind blow against me
excited to get it over with
happy
I paced along the board thinking, "I'm going to do this" over
   and over in my mind
sunburn
hot
excited

With this list, Jenny was ready to draft.

First drafts are often prose or proselike. That is to be expected. The students' experience is prose. Only a gimmick like Koch's makes most students' early drafts sound poetic. My job, and that of the peers, is to help the student work from prose to poetry. We do it by holding conferences about the poem, talking about the feeling the poem created in us, the strong images, the words that call attention to themselves. As a class we discuss first lines, the sense of poetic endings as compared to story endings, the differences in reader responsibility in poetry and prose, the effect of detail. The discussions aren't prescriptive but sustain a heightened awareness of the choices that writers make and the consequences of those choices. In the process of discussion, and in successive drafts, most kids move from prose toward poetry.

Jenny's early drafts are fairly typical. Her first draft simply retells the story with no poetic devices.

> the water just stood there looking at me
> the wind was whistling in my ears
> I took one small step and another glimpse
> at the water made my stomach spin
> my heart was thumping in my
> ears my hands tight to my sides
> another step, splash

In conference I asked Jenny's partner to tell her the feeling the poem evoked. I then asked Jenny to think about the feelings she wanted to evoke. She decided on nervous, happy, and scared. With that in mind, she wrote her second draft.

> the water just stood there looking at me
> the wind whistling in my ears
> I noticed some kids below yelling and screaming
>   my stomach fluttered
> I took a small step and then another a gaze
> at the water made my stomach spin
> Inside a lump was forming in my throat
> my hands tight to my sides
> I felt my body tighten
> I then felt my eyes slowly close

> Another small step   I felt nothing below my
>   feet I was in the air my stomach
>   spinning so fast I thought I would fly
>   away like a helicopter   splash
> A smile grew across my face
> the lump in my throat grew smaller and
> returned to normal size

She had tried to convey her identified feelings to her readers without using the words directly. But it still didn't feel like a poem to Jenny or her partner. She returned to the "what makes a poem a poem" list that we had generated. After reviewing it she wrote a third draft:

> the strong (deep) blue of the water
> looked up at me urging me to [go on]
> I shivering (ed) the breeze whistling
> in my ears. I had to jump. I had to.
> I gazed at the sparkling water on this beautiful (blue)
>   summer morning the sun
> like a spotlight right on me   I had to jump. I had to.
>   I took a small
> step and then I leaped off the board,
> splash. A smile grew across my face. I
> was sparkling like the water.

Although she had used comparisons in the second draft, they didn't really help evoke a feeling. Her comparison in the last line of this draft does. And she used repetition effectively, compounding the feeling of compulsion: she had to dive. In her fourth draft she started to work on her line breaks, moving further away from prose writing. She kept most of her lines from the third draft, and added several more.

> I THINK I CAN, I KNOW I CAN, I DID
> The deep blue water
> looked up at me on the blue summer morning
>   urging me to go on
> I shivered
> The breeze whistling in my ears

> I had to jump
> I just had to
> I gazed at the sparkling water
> on this blue summer morning
> The sun
> light a spotlight right on me
> I had to jump
> I just had to
> I took a small step
> I leaped off the board
> Splash
> I had to jump
> I just had to
> A smile grew across my face
> I was sparkling like the water

She repeats her phrase about having to jump three times in this draft. She has let go of any reference to her stomach's spinning and the lump in her throat. There is still a chronology as she moves down the board, but the focus is now on the water, the sky, and inner thought. In her last draft she kept her wording and line breaks, but changed the title to "On a Blue Summer Morning." Through the drafts you can see how Jenny has gone from an essentially prose account toward poetry: from retelling to presentation. In the process, she used certain concepts that the class identified as functional aspects of poetry. She chose, too, to disregard others. The piece works as a poem, evoking a physical scene, a sense of nervous pressure, and the exhilaration of risking and succeeding.

Another Approach

The next year I added one more step to the students' rehearsing for the final draft. Borrowing (stealing, really) an idea from Don Murray, I had my students layer drafts of their poem to try to get them to extend the amount of drafting so that they would work for stronger images and language. What is layering? After doing their brainstorming, they wrote a draft, put it away, and the next day wrote a second draft without looking at the first one. They wrote drafts for three successive days, then looked back at all their drafts and started to craft a finished poem. Here are Ashley's drafts and final poems. It is interesting to see how information and ideas are present in some drafts and not in others. She clearly works through a number of ideas, images, and words in developing her poem.

Here is Ashley's first draft:

> A sudden Fall with a crash
> She slid on the clear ice like a baseball player sliding into home plate
>   Stop Stop Stop
>   Help Help Help
> The black bar came towards me like a tremendously
>   Big ball coming at me
> Everything was blurred.
> BANG
> A sudden taste of dirt and blood came into my mouth
> I still heard the scratching and screeching of my boots on
>   the ice that sounded like long nails on a chalkboard.
> It seemed endless.
> Then it Stopped
> Everything went blank.

Ashley's second draft:

I fell like a dead bird falling from the sky.
A sudden shiver down my back hit me like a bolt of lightning.
  Stop
  Stop
  Stop
  Help her
  Help her
  Help her
The screeching and scratching of my boots on the ice were like
    long nails scratching endlessly on a chalkboard.
Then it stopped.
My mouth hit a big black thing like a baseball hitting a glove.
A taste of dirt came into my mouth. And the blood added to it.
I slipped like a baseball player sliding into homeplate.
Suddenly everything went black.

Her third draft:

I fell like a dead bird falling from the sky.
Sliding on the ice with great speed I was like a baseball player
    sliding into homeplate.
    Stop
    Stop
    Stop
My boots screeched and scratched like long nails scraping on a
    chalkboard endlessly.
    Scratch
    Scratch
    Scratch
Then it stopped!
The black bar came towards my mouth like a baseball hitting
    a glove.
A sudden taste of dirt came into my mouth. Then blood
    Scratch
    Scratch
    Scratch
The scratching started again.
I started slipping. I was falling again
Everything went blank.

Her fourth draft:

I slipped and fell off the wooden post Kerplunk like a dead bird
    falling from the sky
A shiver down my back hit me like a bullet just shot out of
        a gun
Stop, . . .
Glide
Stop . . . Glide
My boots screeched and scratched as I skidded on the ice sounding
    like long nails scratching endlessly on a chalkboard.
Scratch
Scratch
Scratch
Stopped!
My mouth hit a big black bar like a baseball hitting a glove

A sudden taste of dirt came into my mouth and thick blood
    added to it.
I slipped like a baseball player sliding into homeplate!
Suddenly crash of my head hitting ice everything went black
    and tears filled my eyes.

Finally, Ashley's final draft:

THE PLAYGROUND BLUES
Slipping off a short wooden log.
A quick drop and then
    Kerplunk!
My boots screech and scratch as I skid across the frozen sand
I steady myself, boots scratching like long nails on a blackboard
    Scratch
    Scratch
    Scratch
My mouth collides with the tightrope bar
A sudden taste of dirt and blood
My legs now out in front, I slide like a baseball player going
    into home
I'm out at the plate. My head hits tears come
freezing in the lines of my face.

Writing the successive drafts helped Ashley move closer to the experience and to feelings about it. In her final draft she lets the incident speak for itself, at the same time getting some distance from the actual incident. Only in the final draft could she make light of the accident in the title—"Playground Blues"—and being "out at the plate."

Taking Time For Words

Once students begin to get a feel for poetry, we work to extend the use of rhyme, rhythm, and word choice. We talk about ways of having conferences with each other: listening to the sounds, the sense; helping each other reach for more. Realistically, much of the spur to find more effective language must come from me. While they have begun to sense that support can be found in criticism as well as praise, most of the students' responses to each other lack any real push. So it is my task to encourage them to find a better word, an extended metaphor, a stronger image.

There is no science to it, only art. I was comforted to read Donald Hall's (1988) description of critiquing work in progress with fellow poets. There is usually no unanimity of sentiment over a piece or the ways to strengthen it; comments may lead either to light or darkness. His description shouldn't have surprised me, but it did. As always, I wanted some assurance that at some level we can know. But we can't. We not only write out of experience but respond from there as well. So my pushing sometimes leads to breakthroughs, other times to resistance. The push grows out of the potential I see in the words and the student's thoughts. I can't just push to push; I have to have a sense, which I seldom reveal, of where the piece could grow. The clearest example I have of a successful push occurred with Jeb, who had chosen to write about the moment he came in second place in our school writing contest. His initial drafts had all the sensory data to show anticipation and disappointment commingled. But it remained particularized, with no clear sense that that was the way of the world, not simply the problem of one ten-year-old boy. I asked Jeb to try to find a comparison that would capture his feeling. He was disappointed in me, or more accurately in my reaction. His partner had said that he was all set. But he begrudgingly accepted the push. For the next three days he tried out and discarded various analogies. Frustrated, he nonetheless became interested in trying to find a comparison that worked. Finally he settled on:

> My hopes which had risen
> began to fall to the ground
> For I was good enough to be honored
> but not enough to be crowned.

In those last four lines he universalized the experience, capturing the feeling of that moment not just for himself, but for all of us. He might not have found it, he might not have succeeded, but he still would have had a clearer sense of what poets and poems do. I doubt that Jeb would or could talk about his poem as I just did, analyzing why it works more effectively this way. But he knew his final draft was more effective. In part he knew from my reaction, but also from his peers and his own sense of accomplishment. He had not settled for, in Donald Hall's terms, a McPoem. Granted, he didn't put in the months or years poets often do to create the poem they want. But he is moving in that direction. Three days on four lines: a process where the work controls time, not the reverse.

Here is Jeb's poem:

THE CONTEST
Quiet quiet hushed the teacher,
Your grade is next.
The announcer's voice boomed loud,
And threatened the air like
An overhanging cloud.
Applause filled the air,
And I immediately heard my name.
My palms became sweaty,
My blood rushed to my face.
But my hopes that had risen
Began to fall to the ground
For I was good enough to be honored
But not enough to be crowned.

While I distinctly remember Jeb's grappling to find the words to say what he felt, I remember other poems where students worked just as diligently to capture an experience—for example, Sara's car crash:

I squeezed my stuffed seal,
though I was shaking,
the brakes were screaming,
my eyes shut
the engine roared,
as the wheels lost the slippery road my stomach turned.
Crack!
lines grew larger and larger in the windshield as if an eye were
        forming in the snow.
Crash!
my window broke, the car turned
rapidly, I crawled from my terrifying prison.

Eric's ordeal as a catcher:

Headed straight for me.
Like a white

Bullet. Sweat dripping down
My face. Mouth dry.
My face in a miniature
Jail.
Boom! Boom!
It echoed in my head like a
Gun shot.
It sent me flying
Backward
I landed on the ground
Like a collapsing bridge
Not knowing what had happened
I got up like a snail
Adjusting my shell.

David playing paddle ball at the beach:

Diving down to the soft white sand,
Like a pelican diving for fish.
Hearing the waves crash near my feet
Soothes my ear as I, as I, as I get closer and
Closer to my dad and the ball
Splat! right next to the shore
The ball is like a frying egg
And me, I ended up as the spatula.

Why Poetry?

Why do poetry? Especially given my own shortcomings, why teach poetry, or have students write poetry? I am not looking to create poets. I want to help children become adults who are effective users of the language—effective more than correct. Recently I attended the wedding of friends. As it was the second marriage for both, their children from each previous marriage formed part of the wedding party. When the time for toasts came, the groom's teenage daughter wanted to propose a toast, but could only manage to sing the first verse of "Feelin' Groovy." The words did not match either her sentiments or the importance of the moment. But her choice suggests how much more comfortable we are choosing someone else's created piece over our own. That is precisely what greeting cards do. No matter how many times I've searched, I've yet to find a card that says what I want to. But then, why should it? It wasn't written by me for the occasion. We've ceded too much to popular culture. If we allow it, through song and word, to speak for us, not only will the words fall short of the experience, but the words and images start to define the experience, altering even what we sense. So I have my students write poetry, staying true to experience and realizing that they can, with work, find their own words for what they feel. In so doing I hope that the experience they are writing about is enriched.

I teach poetry for other reasons as well. Lucy Calkins does an excellent job in her book *The Art of Teaching Writing* (1986), of pointing out how some students express themselves better in one genre than another. My experience corroborates hers. Specifically, I have had several students who were unable to write sustained pieces, but who wrote poetry tellingly. Kilian was the clearest example. He struggled with prose pieces, feeling frustrated and inadequate. I required him to have those prose experiences, to struggle to express himself, or at least to make himself understood. But his voice was poetry, the poetry of Shel Silverstein. Not only had he imbibed Silverstein's verse, but in it he found a kindred soul. And that kinship let him speak:

> VII
> They say the world was made in seven days,
> To make all the oceans, mountains, and bays.
> But I don't believe that stupid lie,
> Because it took eight days for my broken globe to dry.

I cannot do all genres within a school year. But I must provide a variety of experiences so that students can find their individual voice. Couldn't it be argued that students can find that voice—that sense of self—on their own? Perhaps what they need is the freedom to explore with support. That point can and has been argued, but I disagree. That kind of nativism or naturalism overlooks the psychology of experience. I did not choose to write poetry for many years. The risk of trying something so foreign to me was too great. Many of our students feel the same way. I waited thirty-three years to experience the power of poetry, to create rather than analyze. We must ask our students to try poetry for what it offers. In doing so, we must structure the experience to provide help and support. Without restricting too tightly, we can provide extensive models and modeling, and rich discussion that draws out the salient features of the models. There is no stronger testament to this approach than Christopher Nolan, the Irish spastic-cum-poet. He documents in his autobiography, *Under the Eye of the Clock* (1987), that his poetic stirrings lie not in his pre-existent soul but in the daily contact with the language of his father. The poems and stories of his father reside now in him. And from those he pieced together how he wanted to speak to the world. That is what I want to offer my students: a word-rich environment that may quicken their language sensibilities, and the need to write out of experience.

A Teacher's Reprise

On reflection, I return to Miss Sawicki's efforts to introduce me to poetry. In addition to Joyce Kilmer's poems, she also had us read Kipling's *Gunga Din*. Though I haven't looked at it in thirty years, I still remember "You're a better man than I am, Gunga Din." In her sentimentality Miss Sawicki paid attention to words that moved her. She didn't ignore poetry, or present it as an academic subject to be held at arm's length. She offered it to us and let it breathe. Perhaps my appreciation of Hughes, Frost, and cummings is just as sentimental as her love of Kilmer. Why not teach Pound or Ferlinghetti? Through my own changing sensibilities I try to help my students appreciate what can be done with language. Jenny re-experienced her sense of accomplishment of going off the high dive in her poem; she also came to realize, unthought of before the poem's being written, a relationship between herself and the water: the water first looking at her and then she sparkling like the water. These are not someone else's thoughts and words; they're her own.

· 4 ·

Shorter Bus Routes: Developing a Persuasive Writing Assignment

> Different topics raced through my mind [of] things I want changed in our school. My pencil had trouble keeping up with my thoughts. (Tim)

Shaping the persuasive writing assignment to engender Tim's degree of involvement took years, years of experimenting and learning on my part. The assignment began almost by accident, when I decided to publish a fifth-grade magazine. Feeling that such a publication should express opinions as well as present stories, poems, riddles, and artwork, I asked all my fifth graders to write a persuasive piece. I gave them a time frame and naively sat back, awaiting the results. Most pieces were weakly conceived and badly written: unformed and unfocused, many lacked even a position. They were written about the weather, disarmament, or little-understood political issues. Many seemed to awkwardly restate parental political positions. Disappointed with the results of this first attempt, I did learn from one of my students. Tris wrote a strong, convincing editorial:

> The Ray School fifth grade playground is in very poor condition. The basketball nets on the blacktop are bent and battered. True

one is still straight, but its net and goal are gone, rendering it useless. The other one has its net there, but it tilts at a crazy angle making it almost impossible for kids to shoot. I am not saying that we should get a pair of basketball nets right away, as I am aware that this costs money, but the nets have been like this for two years! I think the school board should reach back into their childhood and see if they think they would have liked their playground equipment like that!

Tris obviously had considerable language facility, which helped make the piece strong. But so did others, and their pieces failed. As I gave Tris's more thought, I realized that the topic had a great deal to do with his success. Tris was writing out of experience. That meant that he knew his topic and felt strongly about the issue: a position that writers need to be in to write well.

First Steps

Since that first year, I have restricted the persuasive writing topic to writing about school or school-related issues (i.e., buses, extracurricular activities, the length of the school day, etc.). Most of my students know of a number of school practices that they want to change, and they feel strongly about them. I restrict the topic not for the sake of restriction, but to make the assignment a better assignment: a richer experience for the students. I've also realized why the restriction works not only to make the writing better, but also to make the writing process more of a learning experience.

Here is a list done by Topher when he was in fifth grade:

- No seatbelts (to remove the seatbelts which had just been installed in the buses)
- No chorus (to end chorus as a fifth-grade elective)
- School start at 9:00 A.M. and end at 2:30 P.M. (at the time school started at 8:00 A.M. and ended at 2:45 P.M.)
- Keep dream bedrooms (a math unit to design and execute a scale drawing of an imaginary bedroom)
- No French (to end the three twenty-minute-a-week French classes)

- Sit together at lunch (to be allowed to sit with friends at lunch instead of being required to sit at your own desk)
- Snowballs (to be allowed to throw snowballs at recess)
- Tackle football (to be allowed to play tackle football at recess and not just touch football)

In giving them the assignment I tell students that everything connected with school is a possible topic. They can argue to keep something as well as to change something. Hence, Topher's list includes keeping dream bedrooms, one of the fifth-grade math projects.

Focusing the assignment made a difference in both process and product. But I needed to do more to make the experience more comprehensive for my students.

> Today I started to write off one of the three beginnings to the writing but I was having a little problem trying to continue but I looked at my lists of positive things and finally got back to writing. (Colin)

At first our brainstorming had been as undirected as the assignment's topic. I gave the students time to plan, explore, think—prewriting with no shape. As I began thinking about the students' lack of nonnarrative experience, I realized the need for more structured prewriting activities. Through modeling—reading persuasive pieces (not standard editorials, but letters to the editor)—students can identify the salient features of persuasive writing. Two important features are arguments for and against the stated position. These two features have become the focus of our prewriting work. The students first brainstorm arguments for their position. Then they explore arguments against, with responses. In both cases they brainstorm alone and then try to extend their list by meeting with a self-selected partner. The exercise gets them to discover what they know about the topic. In the process they develop a better feel for their position. I have had a number of students stake out a position only to surrender it as they begin to consider the counterarguments.

Topher chose to write about snowballs at recess. Here are the lists he and his partner came up with:

Arguments for:
- It's our bodies
- They're fun
- Great to have them on Playspace [a large wooden playground structure]
- Only in winter which isn't long
- Our fault if we get hurt

Arguments against with solutions:
- Sort of dangerous   Answer: Be careful
- Innocent bystanders may get hurt   Answer: Be careful
- No designated field   Answer: Make one
- No room   Answer: Use the place behind the school down the hill
- Kids may put rocks in the snowballs   Answer: Snowball monitor (teacher)

Theirs is not a long list or a particularly strong one. But the important point is that it is a structured beginning. In retrospect, I'm rarely impressed with my own early brainstorming on a topic. What's important is that it gets the writer moving into the piece. Fortunately one doesn't need to get it right the first time. The list making helps move students into a piece much more actively than simply asking them to do some planning. I'm well aware that there are many different planning strategies and that listing may not work for all my students. But I want them to experience a number of different techniques so they can choose the strategies that work best for them.

Colin's statement in his journal entry ("I was having a little problem trying to continue but I looked at my lists of positive things and finally got back to writing") suggests that the lists help not only in uncovering information, but also by serving as a prompt during the actual drafting. How often we forget points that we want to make or information that we have. The lists can help create movement and sustain it.

Becca helped me write my first draft, like I wanted her to—sounding like I was talking in an argument. I found that writing my three beginnings were pretty easy, probably because I had already planned mine out.

I also wrote a fourth beginning before I did my draft and I liked it much better. Probably because it had a way to it, it wasn't exactly saying what I want to happen fiercely, but not calmly either.(Erica)

Another important step in developing purposeful prewriting experiences was to have my students write multiple leads. Multiple leads allow them to surrender the idea of first draft–final draft, a compelling notion that is difficult to give up. But it is an important notion to surrender, because it releases the writer from the pressure of getting it right from the beginning. That release is evident in Erica's journal entry. Not only did she write three beginnings, but she realized that none of them worked to her satisfaction. So she wrote a fourth one as the beginning of her draft. Only by doing the first three could she find one that had "a way to it," balancing the fierce and calm tones to her satisfaction.

Topher went through the same process with his drafting. He wrote three leads and then, through conferencing, came up with a fourth that did the job better than the other three. Here are his three prewriting leads followed by the first-draft lead:

- I've thought about this a lot and I think that I have a plan. The plan is the following. We could use the place behind the school and down the hill. It's the place where we play capture the flag in P.E.
- "Please can we have snowballs? They're fun—really fun," I said.
  "No Johnny, someone may get hurt!" said Mr. Johnson.
  "Ya, but we'll be really careful," I whined.
  "No, Johnny, I said no!"
  "Please, Mr. Johnson."
- "Nanana booboo you can't get me!"
  "Oh ya!" As the snowball whizzed through the air, it hit Joey in the head. He stumbled and fell. His head had fallen onto a rock.
- I think that we should have snowballs, because they're fun, actually they are really, really fun. Plus it's our bodies, so if we get hurt it's our fault. Also the snow only comes in winter and early spring which isn't the whole school year.

Topher's early leads show a willingness to experiment. But in writing his leads, Topher buried his position. Only in his draft lead, arrived at through conferences, did he recover it: allowing snowballs at recess. Before I incorporated this step of writing multiple leads into the prewriting part of the assignment, I got many persuasive pieces with confusing or ambivalent beginnings. Writing multiple leads gave Topher, Erica, and their partners the opportunity to listen and think through what they wanted to say and how they wanted to say it. They could then come up with a beginning that has a "way to it." Topher's isn't a strong beginning, but it's much stronger than his first attempt.

Our prewriting for this genre now has a specific structure: brainstorm topics, brainstorm arguments for and against, and write multiple leads—a substantive change from that first year of simply giving the assignment and waiting for results.

Oral And Written Persuasion

As I walked into L.A. different thoughts raced through my mind as other students said "It's fun, you'll like it." We always told each other what was ahead in each class.

I scanned the board as I thought about different words that appeared on the board: blackmail, beg, puppyface. What in the world are we doing today?
We talked about a piece of writing we had done [for homework].

I had enjoyed it. We had to write about a time our parents said "no" to something and somehow we had changed their minds. (Tim)

Having developed the prewriting phase, I began to look for experiences in students' lives that could enrich the first stages of the persuasive writing assignment. I realized that the students had some knowledge of persuasion. All of them were continually trying to persuade others orally to do things. Helping them realize that, and placing oral and written persuasion on a continuum, makes it possible to better understand the conventions necessary for written persuasion. Tim, in the excerpt from his journal given above, alludes to the most popular forms of oral persuasion: begging and histrionics. Other popular strategies are arguing from fairness, picking opportune moments, and bargaining. As

Tim mentioned, I now have students write about an experience when "our parents said 'no' to something and somehow we had changed their minds." I have them do this before we begin to read or write persuasive pieces, before the final writing assignment is even discussed. Emily's example is fairly typical of the response:

> "Please Mom," I begged, "can't I stay up until nine?"
>
> "You go to bed at 8:30 P.M. or you can't wake up at 6:30," said my mother sternly.
>
> I pretended to choke back tears until my mother asked, "What's the problem? Are you behind in your school work? Is that what's bothering you?"
>
> I shook my head.
>
> "Has someone been picking on you?" my mother questioned.
>
> I shook my head again.
>
> Finally she asked, "What's the trouble? Is it your bedtime?"
>
> I nodded pretending to be more upset then ever.
>
> "Sweetie," my mother said tenderly, "you know you will be exhausted if you stay up til nine and get up at 6:30."
>
> "But Mom," I said, sounding very upset, "I never go to sleep 'til nine anyway, and from 8:30 to 9 I start worrying about things. I start getting pains in my stomach and think that I have some horrible disease. . . ."
>
> "O.K.," my mother said, "you can read until nine, but if your eyelids begin to feel droopy don't hesitate to turn off the light."

Emily begged, pleaded, used body signals, and presented evidence to dispute the advantages of the earlier bedtime. By starting at this point I get students to realize the differences and similarities in oral and written persuasion. Begging and pleading don't work in written form. Yet without this discussion, many students resorted to begging in their papers. You can see it, for instance, in Topher's second lead in his snowball argument.

Having students consider their oral arguments also helps them realize that they have several voices, not just one. Often I have them write a separate description of a time they persuaded a sibling. In this piece they are much more forceful, especially if the sibling is younger. Realizing that their voice changes with the audience helps them as they work on their persuasive piece, which will be addressed to the principal. They discuss with their partner the tone of the piece. Not only can they not beg, plead, or use too much force, but they also must find a correct distance from their audience. How much deference must they show? How should the facts be phrased? These questions can be related to the students' use of language in oral persuasion.

Michael found it difficult to sit still in class. Often abrasive and judgmental, he seldom considered the feelings of others. He would simply react. But he understood that he could not come across that way and hope to persuade the principal to change the rule about not running on Playspace. He worked hard to make his case deferentially, but not obsequiously; forcefully, but patiently:

Dear Mrs. McLaughlin,

I just got in from recess and I will tell you one thing: I am not the least bit out of breath, and the reason for this is that I didn't run all recess long.

Of course you can run off Playspace but there isn't any fun in it and most kids go outside to have fun. I am sorry if I'm acting a little pushy but after you have gone all day without running and all day with all that energy in your system, you tend to get this way. Not being able to run also affects your work because you have all that extra energy bottled up inside you and you tend to get very jumpy.

I realize that children tend to get hurt but I have a solution. We could put up signs all over Playspace that said:

SLOW DOWN
SPEED LIMIT 3 MILES PER HOUR

And others similar to it. If this does not work, I have another idea: We could have fifth grade patrol guards much similar to lifeguards. A class would take turns every week. Every day different kids would be assigned. Every recess they would do things like shout "Slow down" if they saw two kids about to run into each other, and try to make sure that no one got hurt. My last point is that there is no point in having recess if you can't run because recess is suppose to be our time and also suppose to be fun and you can't have real fun if, well . . . have you ever tried to play tag walking? I know that you will make the right choice.

Originally I read the students only a few examples of persuasive writing, culled from letters to the editor in my local newspaper. As I began to realize how little experience the children had had with written persuasion, I started to read them persuasive pieces written by fifth graders from prior years. At first I read only successful pieces, ones like Michael's above. Then I realized that a better way to show them the importance of language would be to read them pieces where the student misspoke. B.J. argued that the students should have a soda machine. She realized that some parents would object. She handled the issue this way:

> There are some people who want their children to get no cavaties (like in the ads) and say "No." So those children who are unfortunate enough to have a parent like that won't have it.

The students' reaction to B.J.'s assertion is my own. The word "unfortunate" turns me against the writer and the piece. In successful work, the seams don't show. The students know that the piece works, but not necessarily why. Sometimes I can help them more by showing the seams.

Working On Endings

> I worked hard and finished the middle of my paper and hustling I wrote my first and second endings. We had been asked to write three beginnings and three endings. . . . I worked quickly and well today. I wrote my last ending and realized how very strong my endings were. (Tim)

Endings are important in all writing. Often they are difficult to isolate and work on. After requiring multiple beginnings, I felt that the students could also benefit from creating multiple endings. First, it would help them realize that there is more than one way to end a piece. Second, they would discover that some endings are stronger than others. Third, they would be released from the pressure of having to get it right the first time.

Topher's endings to his snowball piece show growth through elaboration.

- Maybe we could have a two week trial period to see how it works. So that's about it, you have reasons why we should have snowballs and reasons why we shouldn't but I've tried to answer them and I *hope* you agree with me.
- And have you ever tried playing snowball in three inches of mud and water with no boots. It's a lot easier to have a snowball fight, but we can't now.
- Maybe we could have a two week trial period. Also let me tell you how it's like out at recess. If we can't play football because it's too wet, and we can't play kickball because they're trying to flood it, and we are bored of Playspace, what can you do? You can have a snowball fight if people would let us.

In Topher's second and third endings you can hear echoes of Michael's strong ending. Strong endings come from working on endings. Initially I didn't give students the opportunity; I expected implicitly that they would get it right the first time, or know how to revise. Building in multiple endings has helped them realize possibilities while they are drafting.

In Allison's persuasive piece you can see the growth of a strong ending. Her piece about bus routes is reproduced below including her three endings in the order that she developed them. Through her final endings you can see her discover a way she can use the ending to take the reader back to the beginning—to tie up the piece. That didn't come out in her first or second attempts. She needed to write through those endings to discover the one that worked better.

Calling America that's what the . . .

The radio blasts out loud and clear on this Tuesday morning and I desperately grope around on the top of my alarm-clock radio to find the volume and restore piece and quiet to my small room. The night before I had been up till 9:00 finishing my homework and hadn't been able to get to sleep until 10. That leaves 8 hours and 7 minutes of seemingly short but treasured sleep.

"Why wake up at 6:07 to get to school at 8:15" you may ask. I wasn't going jogging.

I don't get to school early either. In fact, I often get to school a bit late. Bus 2 comes to my stop at 7:20, and I get to school at 8:15.

That's almost a whole hour on the bus, and by the time I get home in the afternoon it is 4:00. In the winter there is hardly any time to play outside before it gets dark. And then in fifth grade there is the added problem of homework which has to be done before dinner to get to bed on time to get up in the morning to catch the bus to get to school on time. Some times I feel like the old lady who swallowed the fly.

When you are always in a rush you tend not to do a terribly good job at anything, and you certainly aren't going to love school if it means getting up at the crack of dawn to sit in a smelly bus for an hour.

So what could you do about this? Well, you could take three crowded buses and split their routes among four buses. Then you have four shorter bus rides. The organization would not be hard and the benefits would be worth the trouble.

As for the cost of the buses, you would only need one or two, and the money from recycling cans could be used. We could cut down on other school expenses. There must be something that is not absolutely necessary.

After all which is better, a bunch of unhappy students and crowded buses that go around in loops with people who have been on for the whole ride waiting for the moment when they can get off, or just one or two extra buses and happy contented students who aren't tired and disappointed about going to school every day?

Allison's first ending:

Changing the routes can't be that hard, and with the increasing amount of students it will be worth it in the long run. And when kids have time in the morning to wake up, and more sleep, they're bound to feel happier and perform better in school. You may not think that there is a problem but for people that have to get up at the crack of dawn to get to the bus on time . . . well, right now they're all trying to catch a few extra winks on the school bus.

Allison's second ending:

I hope you agree in the long run the one or two extra buses that we could get right now would definitely be worthwhile, especially with the increasing number of students. And the school performance of the students who would be able to get enough sleep and be HAPPY about going to school in the morning.

Allison's third ending (and the chosen ending for the piece):

So now as I roll over and try to forget that it is a school day, I wonder why no one has done anything about the long bus rides. It would not be hard to re-do one or two bus routes and it would be well worth every bit of effort to have students who are happier about school and who are not too tired to do their best. With the increasing number of students the few extra buses WOULD get their full use. Let-t-t's begin again . . .

Calling America! That's what the . . .

I rolled over in my bed and looked at the clock. It was 7:00. That was a nice sleep. Time for a wonderful day of school! I smiled and looked out my window. It was sunny out, and I knew this was going to be a good day. I jumped out of bed full of excitement and vigor, ready for a new day.

Given the time and the opportunity to confer, a chance to reflect, Allision found an effective way to make her ending stronger. She recaptured a specific image, which tied the piece together. Conferences often play a critical part in making written work effective.

Conferences

Before I met with Mr. Wilde (or Mrs. Williams) to look over my persuasive piece, I underlined a few words I thought were important. I also took away (crossed out) a few words and added some. I read it after I did that, and it sounded very good. I also got Becca [her peer editor] to read it out loud to me, so I could sort of be in Mrs. Murphy's [the principal] position and added a few words I thought were important for the reader, or in my case, the listener. I hope I'm ready for the final. . . .

I met with Becca again before I met with Mr. Wilde. She said it was still a bit fast and to put in even more detail! She said it was mostly straight and fast in the fund raising part. I tried to put in more, but just couldn't. (Erica)

Students serve as peer editors not only at the beginning of the piece, in prewriting, but throughout the project. Originally I was the students' only editor. The third year we started to share some works in progress as a whole class. Several years ago I had each child choose a peer partner to confer with throughout the project. Erica describes well what her partner did for her in helping Erica strengthen her persuasive piece about reinstating the fifth-grade musical. Becca pointed out that the piece moved too quickly, that it needed more detail to make the points stronger. In a subsequent journal entry Erica wrote, "I added a part about when we practice the fifth grade musical."

We spend time as a class and in individual conferences discussing how to make our pieces effective. The following issues are often raised:

- Do I state my position in the first sentence?
- Where do I use my strongest reason for or against?
- How many arguments and counterarguments should I use?
- How should I end the piece?
- What kind of examples should I give?

The discussion is always rich. There are no right and wrong answers, only considerations to be weighed in creating an effective piece. This past year a boy argued convincingly to his classmates that the piece should have one less counterargument than reasons for, so that the balance of the piece tipped in favor of the position. It didn't become a rule for persuasive writing, but it did become another point to consider. And very often the changes that come out of those considerations occur days later in another draft or another piece. So although on the day Erica made her journal entry she couldn't add anything more, later on she could.

Erica also had Becca read her piece aloud in order to get some distance from her own writing, making her better able to imagine how her intended audience would receive it. Here is the piece that Erica ended up writing with Becca's help:

FIFTH GRADE MUSICAL

All kids should have a chance to act. If we have a fifth grade musical this would happen! The fourth grade did "Frankly,

Franklin," so why can't we do a musical? If we had a musical we could use our voices in dramatic ways. It could also help us learn how to memorize long pieces.

We could do a musical about history. If we do that it could be a part of the subject we are working on. It could also teach the audience. Then we could practice during work period.

I know Mrs. Butler (the music teacher) is busy. I'm sure that we could make a schedule to fit her schedule. If we don't have enough money we could do a project like making tee shirts and sell them. We've done it before, let's do it again! We've got a lot of talented kids here, let us show it!

Conferences have helped many students help their peers. In the process they have become more aware of what is and isn't working in their own writing. When I first gave the persuasive writing assignment, students didn't have that opportunity.

Nor was the circle of audience and writer completed in the first years of the assignment. Children wrote persuasive pieces but did not get to share them with their intended audience. For the last two years, however, persuasive pieces have gone to the principal, and she has responded. I can't ask her to read and respond to all seventy papers. Each class self-selects four or five that the principal reads. She then comes into the class and discusses them with all of us. By building it into the assignment, students re-evaluate their writing in the class, and they re-evaluate it for a purpose. As they choose the pieces to go to the principal, the students' comments reflect what they have learned: "not enough reasons," "ending too weak," "strong beginning," "no examples," "too fast," "can't follow."

The persuasive writing assignment has changed dramatically in the nine years I have given it. In the beginning it was an ill-conceived idea with little shape, just an expectation. During these nine years it has taken on various shapes as I have realized what the assignment asks of students and how I can best help them be successful.

The Assignment Now

Through reflection and discovery, the assignment has changed a great deal over the years. Right now the persuasive pieces are developed through the following steps:

1. Students write a one-draft piece describing a time when the child persuaded a parent to do something the parent initially did not want to do.
2. We discuss the art and strategies of oral persuasion, which leads to a discussion of similarities and differences between oral and written persuasion.
3. I read/model persuasive pieces by adults and former fifth graders; we discuss the pieces, to establish the salient aspects of written persuasion.
4. Students receive the assignment: to argue for a change in some practice at school or, alternatively, to argue for keeping some present practice.
5. After discussion of the qualities sought in a good editor, students choose a peer editor.
6. They brainstorm possible topics, alone and with their editor.
7. They choose a topic and generate reasons for their position—alone and with the peer editor.
8. They generate a list of counterarguments.
9. They answer the counterarguments.
10. They write three different leads.
11. At any time, up to this point, a position can be abandoned and a new one developed.
12. Students draft with peer response.
13. They write multiple endings.
14. They go through the process a second time to develop another paper.
15. They choose one of the papers for further revision; they produce a final draft.
16. In groups of four, they evaluate and put forward one or two final papers that the group would like to send to the principal.
17. The class sends four to six papers to the principal. Class time is set aside for the principal to respond in person.

Is the assignment now in final form? No. There are still issues to address. For example, many of the children's pieces would benefit from some research. They know a lot about the subject, but could know more to argue more cogently. They could benefit from being able to better distinguish between position and argument. Often, students choose pieces to send to the principal more on the basis of the paper's position than its cogency. So there is more work to do. I must also balance this assignment with the other projects scheduled for the year. This four-week assignment could easily be expanded to six. Do I want that? What are the trade-offs? I have come a long way in developing the assignment and uncovering its value, but there is more to do.

> Today during all my free time I worked on my writing. I finished writing my Martin Luther King Day piece with an extremely strong ending. . . . My second piece (on better food in the cafe) is not as strong and well written as my first piece. I really like my first piece. (Tim)

Here is that piece about the school honoring Martin Luther King by making his birthday a holiday:

MARTIN LUTHER KING

I am sitting here unhappily, hoping that someday we will celebrate Martin Luther King Day like kids in Washington, D.C., who are having a parade in tribute of him. Not logical would you say, over 40 states celebrate the day, and New Hampshire does not!

I strongly feel that not celebrating the day is truly not right. Look at what he's done: He was the man who led Blacks and other people discriminated against to freedom.

We have never recognized a Black hero in our community. Martin is the perfect idol!

I think Martin Luther King should be known to everyone just like George Washington and Abraham Lincoln. He did as much for the Blacks and other people discriminated against as Washington did for the U.S.

There isn't very much we can do but we must write a letter to our State Representatives because they must know our feelings.

Our State Representatives disagree with the facts by saying that it's better if we just learn about him in school. Seriously, how much do you learn about him every year? The teachers practically teach us the same thing year after year.

We could have a carnival or parade so people will think of him in a positive way. Norwich (our sister district in Vermont) has the day off, why can't we? He should be recognized as an important figure in American history, not some man who some states agree with and some don't. What reasons do we have for not celebrating Martin Luther King Day? It's just not right. He brought about very strong feelings in people to stick up for what is right. We don't have the right not to recognize him. I mean . . . well . . . how would you feel if we didn't celebrate George Washington's birthday in any way?

Tim liked his Martin Luther King Day piece. His class liked the piece too, but did not choose it as one of the pieces to send to the principal. Disappointed, Tim still had a sense of accomplishment.

Colin's piece was one of the pieces chosen. He wrote about Ray School products.

I walked through the front door of the Ray School a little late, and I was hurrying to get to my classroom but suddenly there were all the teachers with Ray School sweatshirts and all the kids had Ray School bookbags.

I wonder how hard it would be to make a few more Ray School products, just a pencil, sweatpants, a hat. Just a few things. It could be fun and bring more pride to our school. Just think of all the kids in the fifth grade who are leaving the school and almost the only thing they have to remember it by are a few memories.

I know that there are some problems. One of the worst is the cost for the products, but really if you think that's easy to solve. You just pay for the products with the money you earn from selling them. Every four years or so a new written and drawn slogan could be chosen. The fifth grade could design them and one could be picked by the teachers. Now you're saying where would we get it printed? All you have to do is find a printing company nearby and get someone to go and pick up the products. Another good thing about this is what happens if someone doesn't have an eraser or a pencil, well if you sold these things kids could use them in school. (The school supplies could have Ray School printed on them.) Another problem is where do you keep them when you're just storing them and where do you keep them when someone buys one? If you're wondering where to store products, just use one of the many school closets, and if someone wants a product they go to the office, ask for something, and someone will go get the buyer what they want. Remember if someone wears or carries a Ray School product somewhere and someone else recognizes the school they might take an interest in our school. Make more Ray School products.

Colin's piece drew a positive response from the principal. She did not agree to set up a store to sell Ray School products, but she did encourage Colin and his classmates to look into setting up a store. The class felt that their words counted, that writing can open up avenues of discussion. With thought, planning, and writing, they could be heard on issues that concerned them. Our students need to know how to present themselves not only in stories, but also in elaborated chains of reasoning. The persuasive writing assignment is one step in helping them see how that can be done.

The first year I gave the assignment Tris's persuasive piece about the condition of the playground was the exception. He knew how to use language and picked a topic that allowed him to craft a well-written piece. I taught him little; he taught me a lot about what fifth graders can do. Topher, Tim, Erica, and Allison benefited from my subsequent shaping of the assignment. My interventions did more than offer a general invitation to try non-narrative writing. They highlighted certain skills and techniques. That made the general quality of the writing—both product and process—better. In retrospect, why didn't I know that when I first gave the assignment? I think because teaching in many ways is like writing: it is a process of discovery. We can't know beforehand exactly where we are going, only the general direction we want to travel. Even given what I know now, the assignment will continue to change as I look for ways to enhance students' understanding and appreciation of non-narrative writing.

· 5 ·

Engaging and Informing: Reconsidering the Written Report

When I began to teach fifth grade there were no set writing assignments in my school save one—a report. It served as the culminating activity for a social studies/science project. I had never asked my third graders to write reports and felt uncomfortable asking fifth graders to do so. Why is report writing so ubiquitous? Should it be?

The Problem

James Moffett accurately, I think, fingered the reason for the pervasive use of report writing: it tests (Moffett 1992). We know from a report whether or not a student has encountered the prescribed material. It is an essay test without the question. From the report we can judge the student's involvement with the information.

Is that bad? Yes. Again Moffett provides the reason: It is "inauthentic discourse," by which I take Moffett to mean that there is no authentic audience aside from the teacher, and no purpose beyond testing. But adults are called on to write reports, so the form must have some validity. Yes, but the purpose of adult report writing is different, and in that difference rests the distinction between the tasks. A business manager requesting a report does not do so to test what an employee knows about the business, but rather to discover something that neither the employee nor employer knew before, nor easily could have come to know without the report. The report isn't a test; it's a coming to know for both writer and reader.

Accepting that distinction, can't it still be argued that testing is a legitimate function of schooling and that writing should be part of that testing? To answer that we must look at the writing process and compare it to traditional report writing. Can students still go through the process in writing a report—choose a topic, prewrite, draft, confer, revise, and produce a final draft? Perhaps. But to do so the child must overcome the tyranny of the texts that provide information—namely, encyclopedias. An encyclopedia is designed to dispense information forthrightly with accuracy, clarity, and conciseness. For most students encyclopedias and encyclopedia-like books are their exclusive written sources. The students are then asked to present this newly gained information in the same way they just received it, but to make it their own. That is hard to do because their sources are such a powerful model of presenting information. Reports then often end up as thinly veiled paraphrases of the original source or a patch job of three or four sources. The only real writing task addressed is how to make someone else's writing sound like your own—not trying on a style in order to learn, but camouflaging someone else's writing for a good grade. There is no new discovery for either the reader or the teacher. The report simply tests.

A Solution

Did I assign reports? Yes. Yes, because I wanted to foster independent learners. Independent learners need to know how to gather, record, and present information. I wanted them to learn those skills while not violating what I was learning about writing. My solution: the end product would still be a written piece, but not a standard report. The piece would reflect the involvement and commitment of the students to a topic and have an authentic audience. But before they write their pieces, I try to engage students with their topic and help them learn how to research.

My students begin their animal research projects in the middle of the year. They spend ten weeks on the assignment, from choosing a topic to making the final presentation. Our projects are on animals because of the intrinsic interest ten- and eleven-year-olds have in animals, and because there is an abundance of appropriate books, magazines, and encyclopedias about animals. To teach research skills we must choose subjects that provide enough sources, so the students are actually doing research and not simply following a well-worn path created by a lack of sources. Students are free to choose any animal they want, with two restrictions: no domestic animals (the information isn't as rich); and only one child in a class can research a specific animal (to eliminate fighting over sources). The librarian and I screen the students' choices, advising those who have chosen rare or obscure animals that they may have difficulty generating facts. The choice of whether to study that animal or not still rests with the students. I want them invested in their topic, studying their choice, not mine.

The first thing I ask students to write is a one-draft list of everything they know, or think they know, before we begin the research. We will use this sheet, their notes, and another list of what they know about their animal at the end of the project to assess what they've learned, not do it through their paper. Next, usually as homework, students come up with forty questions about their animals. I chose forty because I want them to stretch, to reach for questions they don't even know they have. Many groan, but all discover that there are many questions about any topic:

- What does an albino polar bear look like?
- Who is the most intelligent of bears?
- How well do penguins see under water?
- How do penguins make their nests?
- Why do sharks eat their young?
- How do sharks communicate with each other?

We share the questions in class, discover that many apply to all animals, and start to develop categories of information to be pursued. I could give them categories and questions. It would be quicker and might be neater, but that doesn't foster independence, a sense that one can go out and find information on one's own. We start with questions because that is at the heart of most research, questions that we feel a need to answer.

How does this work lead to nontraditional report writing? It doesn't. This work creates the curiosity, the will to know, and gets students thinking about the kinds of things they want to know. I address the issue of report form by reading to them. As with all our other genre work, I model approaches to the assignment. Only this time there isn't one approach, but many. Over a period of weeks, while students work on their categories, learn how to take notes, and begin to take notes, I read them published authors' accounts of animals told in a variety of prose and poetic forms. These are not anthropomorphized animal stories like *Wind in the Willows* but works like *Incident at Hawk's Hill* (Eckert), *The Wounded Wolf* (George), and "A Bat is Born" (Jarrell). As always, we discuss what is effective about each piece, and we raise questions; I also ask the students to list specific information they learn from each piece. Together we discover the wealth of information each contains. With some, we then look at the kinds of information that are contained, using our categories to organize the facts presented. Although not directed to do it yet, the children have been made aware that information can be presented in various forms, not simply in the form of an encyclopedia entry. They hear authentic, informative writing, written to engage as well as inform. They begin to develop their own sense of what can be done to present information. In this context we discuss the standard report. Most agree that the form presents information efficiently but does little else.

In the beginning, unsure of what students could do, I allowed them to choose the form of a standard report or one of a number of options. I no longer give them such a choice. Convinced of the importance of translating the information from one genre to another, I now prohibit the traditional report form. I have seen that they can move beyond it and learn much about writing in the process. So the written assignment is: Write a paper that is both informative and engaging.

Steps In The Process

From the specific reading I've done in class of both professional and student examples, and the students' own general reading experience, we develop a list of approaches to the writing, which usually includes the following:

- Diary, kept by the animal or a researcher.
- Letters, usually between animals.
- Script.
- Story, told by the animal or a human.
- Who Am I?
- Interview.
- "Choose your own adventure" story.
- Poem.

Students are not to anthropomorphize their animal, but for purposes of the paper their animal may speak or write. The children are not limited to the list we come up with; they may use approaches they think of on their own. Many students try out several genres before deciding on a form. The planning and early drafting steps are designed to encourage and support experimentation. The first step is to make an informal outline. Each child has collected at least one hundred facts on the chosen animal. They must present fifty in the paper, so they need to decide which facts they want to present and in what order. They are not wedded to their outline; it simply gets them to make choices and to order them. They take a piece of paper, divide it into three sections—beginning, middle, end—and list the categories they hope to cover in each. Here is Jeb's outline for his cheetah:

Beginning	**Middle**	**End**
Habitat	Breeding/babies	History/future
Feeding	Raising the young	Life span
Behavior	Feeding	Relationship to man
	Abilities	
	Defense	
	Temperment	
	Communication	

Jeb's outline shows that he is deciding which categories to use. He wrote "feeding" in both the beginning and middle slots to indicate to himself that he wants to present information in that category throughout most of the paper.

Next, students write multiple leads, just as they did in the persuasive writing assignment. Here are two of Jeb's leads:

- The female cheetah jumped lazily up on the crooked tree branch. As she scanned the grassy plains of the Serengeti for pray she sprayed the branch with urine to mark her territory.

  She suddenly spied a herd of Thompson's gazelles about half a mile away. She dropped down and started her long stalk.

- Instinctly, I leaped out of the bushes into a fifty mile an hour sprint towards a small Thompson's gazelle. I, a female cheetah, thought, chewing on a huge hunk of meat. Using my tail as a rudder I could turn on a dime. I ran beside the gazelle, knocked him down, and went for the suffocating throat hold.

In his leads, Jeb experiments with several aspects of writing. He tries both the third and the first person. He tries starting with description and with action. He tries beginning with a behavior fact and a skill fact. There is no one right way to start. With the thinking and experimenting, Jeb will make an informed decision about how he will actually start the piece. He could also decide at this point that he did not like the story form and try a completely different genre.

Choosing a genre is an important step, and one often not emphasized in writing assignments. The genre will determine the way in which information can be presented and the ways in which a reader can be engaged. Each student has an assigned peer conferencer who is consulted throughout the writing of the paper. That person is consulted now to help decide whether or not to continue with the chosen genre. The decision must be made within a two-week period so students have ample time to draft. Occasionally I allow students to change genre at a later date, but only after I apprise them of the difficulties they are creating for themselves.

While genre and lead are being chosen and the students begin to draft, we continue to discuss techniques for making the writing work within genres and across them. For instance, we list techniques useful in generating and sustaining a reader's interest. My students develop their own list from the professional and student examples I have read to them. The list usually includes, but isn't limited to, the following:

- Embedding information
- Humor
- Adventure

• Suspense
• Clarity
• Story ending
• Flashbacks

They think of the list and the examples they have heard as they write. For instance, Jeb wanted to present information about the female cheetah and the ordeal she faces in raising her young. About three weeks before Jeb started drafting his story, he had heard me read about a badger digging a den to give birth. After describing the badger's den building, the author presented some information about rearing the young this way:

> Quite soon now, certainly within the next four or five days, her young would be born. They would be her third litter and, with luck, perhaps it would be a litter as successful as the first had been; hopefully not as ill-fated as the second. (Eckert 1971, 34)

Through the use of flashback, Allan Eckert presented problems and patterns in badger rearing. Jeb obviously saw it as a successful technique because he wrote this about a female cheetah:

> One week before she was due she made a small nest in a thorn bush. She was thirty-six months old, and this would be her second litter, and she hoped it would be more successful than the first.

Jeb also used his flashback, as Eckert had, to present information about rearing young cheetahs. Plagiarism? No, because Jeb had heard and dealt with other written material in the interim. It is rather the acknowledgment by one writer that another writer has presented a solution that is worth trying. Jeb is learning to look at not only what writers say but how they say it.

A second source that informs the students' craft is the problems or challenges inherent in the genre they choose. For example, many students initially choose to write interviews. Having developed a list of questions and having answered many of them, the children think that an interview can simply consist of questions and answers. But will that work? No. To maintain a reader's interest the questions must follow from the previous answers, and some kind of interplay must exist between the interviewer and the interviewee. Writers must work on the flow of the interview from question to answer to question and must develop some relationship between the characters. Matt addresses those issues in his paper when a sea lion interviews a shark:

> "The next question is what do you use your teeth for?"
>
> "Well Mr Sea Lion, I use my teeth for biting and tearing not chewing."
>
> "My next question Mr. Shark is can your teeth bite through anything?"
>
> "Well they couldn't bite through an ocean liner but I can bite through a lot of things like wood, rubber, bones, flesh, some kinds of metal, fish, and other sharks."
>
> "That's sure a lot of stuff, Mr. Shark. Can you hold all that in your stomach?"
>
> "Sure I can, my stomach can hold almost anything like nails, cans, glass, metal, flesh, bones, humans, animals, license plates, raincoats, etc."

This brief excerpt shows how Matt has the sea lion go from teeth to biting to ingestion. (The discussion may also suggest what will happen to Mr. Sea Lion!)

The combination of general techniques for maintaining interest and the specific requirements of a genre make for rich conferences on works in progress. Matt not only had demonstrations of the professional authors' ways of presenting information, classroom discussions of techniques, and individual conferences with me, he also met daily with his peer editor to discuss his emerging paper. Because of the framework of the assignment, those conferences were important: the editor needed to let the writer know how much and what kind of information had been presented, and also whether or not the writer was establishing and maintaining the reader's interest. The editor's reactions are important to the writer precisely because the writer is trying to present information to the general public, not just the teacher.

A Sample Paper

The richness of the experience, with its strands of genres and techniques shared and discussed and of papers shared, can be seen in the finished product: a student paper. The following is a story about a dolphin by Brian Ogden. In it he presents much of what he learned about dolphins. As you read it, keep the following questions in mind:

- How is information used in the story?
- What is Brian's relationship to those facts?
- What issues of craft is Brian dealing with?
- What does he know about writing effectively?

HAROLD (A DOLPHIN TALE)

My Younger Years

My mother knew as my wildly splashing tail emerged that this was the birth of an unusual dolphin. She took most careful care of me, especially being sure that my dad or any other male dolphin did not bite me. My swimming was wobbly at first and my tail splashed wildly. I could not breathe without sticking my entire head out of the water. As I grew older, I grew rapidly gaining 18-20 pounds a day just by drinking my mother's milk! I looked like my dad, a bottle-nosed dolphin. I was longer and plumper than the common dolphin; my markings were not as striking. My back was black, almost a purple gray, with my coloring fading to white on my stomach. I soon developed an appetite for cuttlefish, squid, and other small fish. However, I must admit that the first fish I ate gave me a terrible stomachache. By wanting more food it brought me to farther distances away from my mother and therefore the beginning of my adventures.

At the age of 4^1/2 (most dolphins stay with their mothers for only 3 months) I decided to leave my mother and explore the world. When I first set out I thought it was going to be a nice peaceful swim. I was wrong. I started out by heading to the north pole. In the beginning I remembered that my mother had said that I was an "insane child" to even think of going to the north pole. But I was already determined to see how cold it would be and see what it looked like. I soon found that I could swim faster than most fish (about 30 mph or the speed of a herd of thundering elephants) and could glide quickly among them. Then suddenly a long gray object flipped all 440 pounds of me into the air three times and then started babbling. He meant no harm. I caught part of what he said! It went something like this: "Did you hear about all that garbage humans are putting into the water? Whewee, it's grody. I think that sewage looks exactly like humans. You should have seen all the blood when they killed Old Man Blue, the whale."

I left half way through his conversation, but he didn't notice and kept right on talking. Just then I heard a big booming sound. It looked like a blue whale in the distance but I knew it was man-made. I was about to burn out of there when I heard a little voice saying, "Please help me please."

I quickly went to where the voice had been and found a bottle-nosed dolphin (like me) getting smashed by a boat. I swam quickly to her and pushed and pushed her away with all my might. When the ship had finally passed by she had a chance to say something. "Thanks!" she said. "My name is Susan, what's yours?"

"My name is Harold. What parts do you come from?"

"Around Boston," she answered.

I liked Susan right away and found myself doing all my best tricks for her. Soon I invited her to come with me to the North Pole. "When do we leave?" Susan replied.

"Now!"

"I can't, I have to build up some blubber to keep warm," she said sadly.

Then I replied, "Well okay, we'll explore these waters together for awhile."

"Great!" she answered.

Then unexpectedly a whistle sounded and because I was so curious I went towards the sound. Unfortunately I found a human with a harpoon. Quickly I whistled to Susan and we both tried to get away. Before I knew it I was hit in the fin. I tugged and pulled, blood was getting in the water. Finally I pulled as hard as I could and got away. There was one minor problem, however, SHARKS!!!!!!!!!!!!!!!!!

After the blood had gotten in the water the sharks became attracted and started to surround me. A big shark (probably the leader) began inching in on me. I took a wild lunge at the shark's gills and easily killed him. Once the other sharks saw what had happened to their leader they quickly departed the site of their dying leader.

I decided to continue my journey north without Susan. I was enjoying the waters off the Canadian coast and enjoying the fish until one day my luck ran out (or so I thought). I was just swimming along and I picked up some strange noises on my sonar and it aroused my curiosity. So I ventured further to where the noise was coming from. Too late I found myself trapped in a net being hoisted into a boat with a sign on it that read Boston Aquarium. As I was being pulled up I tried my best defense on the men, my stunning clicks (they always worked on other fish). They didn't work on the men at all! I was suddenly aware of men coming at me with a needle.

When I came back to my senses I was in a strangely shaped tub kind of thing with another dolphin in the other corner.

My Years In Captivity

I soon became acquainted with my trainer. Everyday we had some kind of routine. I had to wait for the best dolphin to do his full turn jump high out of the water, then I would use up all my strength to swim on my back. I was the best at that. For some strange reason each time I did a trick my trainer gave me a fish or two. He sometimes sneaked a couple extra fish to me. I had no objections to his behavior. I realized how much easier life was without having to struggle for food, but I also missed my friends in the ocean and the adventures.

I often heard my trainer talking about how intelligent he thought I was. He thought the games that I played with the other animals in the tank were very interesting. I could even solve problems like getting a fish to eat out from under a small rock. I got the fish out by killing a scorpion fish (it is armed with many poisonous spines) and prodded the fish and it came out. He thought it was remarkable that I could solve so many problems and insisted to his friends that I had a great mental capacity. When they laughed at him he got mad and said that a dolphin's brain was about the same size as a human's and that they probably communicate in a language too complicated for us to understand.

For what must have been years I learned many tricks. But one day I found that it was getting harder to do my tricks. I couldn't get nearly as high as I use to on my jumps. I guess it was for this reason I was transported back to the sea.

My Golden Years

I was afraid that I had lost my instincts. As I plunged the full 70 feet my lungs compressed. I hadn't gone so deep in years. It felt great. I stayed down for about 15 minutes. This was the most refreshing dive I had in years. Soon I sighted a school of dolphins, some were bottle-nosed others spotted. As they approached me I sent out my "greetings" communications signal and they clicked to me "Would you like to join our group?" (Dolphins are always friendly to other species of dolphins).

They were on their way to the wedding ceremony of their friends. I had never been to such a ceremony so decided to join them. I found the whole thing incredible. The male and female dolphin perform a beautiful dance. They flash in and out, slowing occasionally to embrace, soaring up into the air, sometimes as high as fifteen feet, and sending a spray up around them like a shower of jewels.

Soon after the ceremony several of the dolphins wanted to swim to the sea of the "Great Blue Dolphin" (actually they aren't blue). We swam for a couple of hours and then started sending out messages for "The Great." When we finally found him they're were already dolphins listening to "The Great's" story of their ancestors. What he said I found very fascinating.

Our ancestors looked like pigs of today. We lived on land like our relatives the whales. Not even "The Great" could tell us why we went to the sea for sure. He thought maybe because of a change in the earth. When we took to the sea our names changed to herring hog, pork pisce and hogfish. This story made me think about my body. I looked at my flippers and my flukes and thought how my body had changed over the centuries. It had adapted from living on land when I had fingers and feet. My blowhole which allows me to breathe must have been a carryover from my ancestors who were air-breathers.

After "The Great" had finished his engrossing story about dolphins I decided to join another group of about 50 dolphins heading for warmer waters (South). I wanted to live out my life with these dolphins, hopefully having an adventure or two.

Brian has successfully addressed a number of issues. For instance, while he adopts a straightforward chronology for telling Harold's tale, and in so doing describes the life of dolphins, he introduces the information about ancestors at the end of the story, when presumably Harold, in his old age, would be more willing to listen and respond to it. Brian isn't bound by his story line to put ancestors first, although strict adherence to species chronology would have forced him to do so. The way he presents information about the dolphin's intelligence is also revealing: the dolphin displays his intelligence in the presence of humans so that they may comment on it. At a story level, Brian has dealt with issues of plot development, although constrained by the information that must be presented. The facts aren't a gloss on the story nor are there separate tracks—story and information; instead, the story is informative and the information has become a story.

But there is much more going on. In writing the story Brian adopts the perspective of the dolphin. This forces him to see the facts through the dolphin's eyes. Thus, right before Harold is captured Brian writes:

> I picked up some strange noises on my sonar and it aroused my curiosity. So I ventured further. . . . As I was being pulled up I tried my best defense on the men, my stunning clicks (they always worked on other fish).

First, Brian uses the dolphin's natural curiosity to advance the story; the dolphin is caught because of a character trait true to dolphins. We, the readers, see what the dolphin is like and the consequence of its inquisitiveness. And then we see the dolphin try to defend itself as it does with other "fish." Here I would argue that we also see Brian standing in a new relationship to a fact. He knows that dolphins use stunning clicks on fish. As he writes his story, taking on the perspective of the dolphin, he wants to defend himself and resorts to what he knows. In so doing that fact comes alive for Brian. It's not just a part of a list of facts but a fact brought to bear on a new situation with an ensuing discovery. ("Oh, so that's why they click when captured.") Notice how he maintains the dolphin's perspective with the parenthetical statement, which signals the dolphin's intent.

Second, Brian not only drives the plot with information, but he embeds that information at the sentence level. He doesn't say that dolphins are curious and that's why Harold swam toward the noise. Rather, Brian shows the noise triggering a natural dolphin response; we learn the fact as it is triggered by an event in the story. The same is true of the stunning clicks; the fact that dolphins use clicks for defensive purposes is embedded in the sentence as Harold reacts to an emergency. On both a sentence and a story level, Brian is synergistically combining information and entertainment.

He does this again when he has Harold listen to "The Great" 's story and then look at his own body, reflecting on what "The Great" has said. Brian knows a lot about writing. He shows what he knows by using adventure to capture the reader's attention. Then he holds the reader by embedding information so that the reader is never pulled out of the story by a fact—the storyteller's spell isn't broken.

Taking Time

Brian's paper took ten weeks from start to finish. Originally I had only allowed six weeks for the project. The students let me know through project evaluations that they needed more time. The research required three weeks to do correctly, and the paper could only be done hurriedly in another three weeks. As I looked more honestly at what I wanted them to do, I increased the time, first to eight weeks, and now to ten. The project is broken down as follows.

The first four weeks:

1. Students choose an animal.
2. They write a pre-research inventory of their knowledge of that animal.
3. They write forty questions.
4. They develop a class category list.
5. They locate and record sources.
6. They research with note taking: they record at least one hundred facts on the animal.
7. I begin modeling genre choices.

The next three weeks:

1. I continue modeling.
2. We discuss approaches to the paper.
3. Students choose a genre.
4. We discuss strategies within and across genres.
5. Students write an informal outline.
6. They write multiple leads.
7. They draft or choose another genre.
8. They solicit peer and teacher responses.

The final three weeks:

1. We conduct final conferences: at least fifty facts must be worked into the body of the paper.
2. Students work on revisions.
3. They write their final draft.
4. They create a bibliography from their source cards.
5. We hold an open house for sharing the writing.

During the last six weeks, in addition to working on the paper, the students also create an art project (a game, an environment board, a picturebook, a puppet play, for examples) using information they have collected. This project serves several purposes. First, it gets the students to translate the information into another form, encouraging them to actively use what they have learned. Second, it provides distance and perspective on their written piece. For instance, while waiting for a conference with me, they spend several days working on their art project. That time away from the paper may let them read it more objectively when they come back to it. Particularly during the final three weeks, they move back and forth between the project and the paper.

How can I spend a quarter of the year on one project? How can I not? Katherine Paterson, the children's author, spends two or three years writing a book. Writing well takes time. I must acknowledge that in the structure of the assignment. The time frames we create send a signal to students. They strive to meet our deadline. If the deadline is unrealistically short, they won't meet their own expectations, or ours. They will feel the shortcoming is their own, and judge their writing ability accordingly.

We must give students time to plan, explore, fail, re-see, distance themselves from the work, and revise. I accept having fewer finished products so that each one can reflect the student's commitment and concerted effort. The results bear out the importance of time. Given the opportunity, students will find effective ways to present their research.

More Genre Options

Not only do the students do well within the modeled genres, but several take me up on the offer to try different genres. When I share those pieces, succeeding classes become convinced that my invitation is genuine, and more students come up with fresh approaches to presenting their information.

Some students, like Aaron, found one genre too limiting. He didn't feel that he could make a diary work on its own. So he decided to write a diary/"Who Am I?" A "Who Am I?" sets up a challenge to the reader to figure out the animal presented. To write a successful "Who Am I?" the writer must order the information from more general to specific. By doing so the writer keeps the reader's interest as the reader continues to try to solve the puzzle. Once the animal has been correctly guessed the impetus to read is gone. Aaron exploited the combination of genres by using the diary as the player in the "Who Am I?" puzzle. That allowed him to present reactions to the puzzle as well as the puzzle itself. The suggestion and choice were his. Two entries give an idea of how he used it:

> Day two: Dear Diary, here's your first clue. One: I have little spikes on my legs to help catch my prey. Two: I like fish for my meals. So do you know it? Well then here's what my day was like. I had fish for breakfast. Then I found my friend Skippy with keen eyes. So we played with each other a little. We play together because he doesn't have a chance. Then we played a game. I'm not sure what you call it, but someone just starts catching fish. Whoever catches the most fish in a certain amount of time wins the game. I'll be back tomorrow.

> Day three: I didn't get much sleep last night because it was pretty windy. Also because the house was shaking a lot. Well, enough of that. Here's your clues for today. Oh yeah, I decided that I'll give

you a few more clues a day because mother said that I can't get a new diary for a looooong time, and I don't want to use the pages up too fast. So here's your clues for today. One: I'm born in an egg. Two: The egg is plain white (no dot or anything like that). Three: My main predator when I'm five years old or older is man, because parts of my body are worth a lot of money. Also they put D.D.T. into our food. That's it for today. I knew it! You don't have a clue on what I am! Do you? This is what my day was like. I did pretty much the same thing I did yesterday, but we didn't have fish for breakfast, we had jackrabbit. Oh shoot I told you another clue. That's all right it wasn't a very big one. Then I started writing to you. I know it wasn't a very big day but I'll write a regular size entry tomorrow. Now I think I'll play with my sister. Bye!

Aaron did not create parallel strands for the diary and the "Who Am I?" He turned the diary into an audience/participant in the "Who Am I?" game. The diary also serves as another means of presenting information, especially the tedium of daily existence, something that could not be presented as effectively in puzzle form.

Every year I think I have seen all available genres. Lulled by a sense of complacency I'm always awakened by some student asking if he or she can use a genre that hasn't even occurred to me—not combining two discussed genres, but going in an entirely new direction. Ariel was one of the first students to do that.

She was a willing student who wrote competently and comfortably for much of the first half of the year. She took few risks, writing stories that followed classroom-modeled patterns. Somewhere in the extended discussion of genres, she must have reflected back on her own reading habits. As we got close to the time to choose a genre she asked if she could do her paper on foxes as a Dear Abby column. Her paper shows that Ariel is well versed in the genre. She knows the tone, length, and kind of responses that are appropriate. She even knows how readers respond to another reader's letter. The following portion of her paper demonstrates her understanding of the genre.

Dear Foxy Loxy,
 I live deep in the woods with lots of animals. We (all the animals) are not getting along. For example, Mrs. Bear is actually letting

her cubs into my den. Now that's not right! Then Mrs. Owl tried
to steal my fox pup. Maybe she does like fox pups, but now?

Confused in the Deep Woods

Dear Confused,

Hold a big meeting with all the foxes. Then talk about what
you should do. I have a few suggestions that you should bring up
at the meeting: 1. You could move to a different place. 2. Call
Mrs. Bear and Owl and discuss things with them!

Ariel knows the genre well. She writes three other exchanges
and then the following:

Dear Foxy Loxy,

I am writing to the fox that signed "Confused in the Deep
Woods." I have had an experience with an owl before, and it's not
fun. The owl took my fox pup. I fought back for it. It did work,
but my fox pup was wounded and so was I, though we are fine
now. We have learned never to go near an owl's nest!

Enemy of Owls

Dear Enemy,

Good idea. I never fought with an owl before, but I'll take your
advice. What a touching story. I'm glad that you learned something from that experience.

Ariel took a risk by using a form that had not been modeled or
discussed in the classroom. But she found power in her choice,
and support from her reading audience.

I often read parts of Ariel's paper to each fifth-grade class. Her
paper has inspired some other Dear Abby's. Others have listened
to her piece and then developed their own newspaper columns.
That's what Torrie did in her newspaper column, Advice for
New (Prairie Dog) Mothers:

Dear New Mothers,

It's spring again. You know what that means! More new babies
and more to learn. For those of you who are new at this, here's a
list of things to expect out of your new born pups. The average
litter is five, but it is not abnormal to range from two to ten. If I
were you I wouldn't be alarmed if I had two.

Your babies may seem small at first, but in two weeks they won't be. When they are born they weigh about a half an ounce. After one week they will gain forty percent, and after two weeks they will gain two and a half times their birth-weight. This all comes from you mothers—your milk.

On day sixteen they start squeaking. It may be annoying at first but you'll get used to it. They do it all the time. On day twenty-one they stand up. They may be a little unsteady at first and you may have to catch them a few times before they get the hang of it.

At one month they start to crawl around the nest. Better move things out of the way or they'll knock them over. A little after that their eyes will open and they start walking. When they open their eyes everything is new to them, even you. When they start walking they can get out of the nest. They may get somewhat curious so lock up the storeroom.

In a couple more days they learn to run and bark. The barking may sound like nonsense to you but soon it will be real communication. When they start running it's a little annoying at first. They run, they learn to jump, they even learn to unlock the locks you've already put up.

At about seven weeks old they've seen everything in the burrow and may want to see more. You can let them pop out of the burrow . . . with supervision of course!

Teaching your pups is no piece of grass. There's a lot to learn and it's up to you to teach it. Communicating is a big thing for them. The fear scream is one signal they may do naturally. If not, teach it. It's one of the most important signals your pup needs. If he's in trouble he can call you.

Don't teach the dispute over food signal too soon, or you may hear too much teeth chattering and too many low growls.

They must learn the two tone alarm bark for when they stick their heads out of the burrow; they may see a predator and have to give the alarm.

Another important thing to teach your pup is what is food and what is not. They may be willing to eat just about anything but that's not always the healthiest thing. Another important thing to teach your pups is which animals to hide from and which are our friends. Without this information you may find yourself in an owl's dinner bowl.

That's all my advice for new mothers this breeding season. Next spring I'll be back again with more tips on raising your pups.

A pup expert

Torrie also took risks. Encouraged by Ariel's piece, she took what she knew about newspapers and the information she wanted to present and invented a column for her *Prairie Times.*

A year ago the fifth grade had an aide whose primary, but poorly paid, job was as an evening news editor for our local television station. As she watched the class work on earlier writing projects, she compared their writing process to her own writing of the eleven o'clock news. We agreed that she should share her experiences and her reflections with the children. She brought in the log sheets that she used, showed the students how she went about writing the news, and explained the process of coordinating written news with videotape footage. A month after her presentation, we started to work on the animal projects. I made no connection between these two events, but Ben did. When choosing a genre, Ben asked if he could do a TV news script. Surprised, I said yes, as long as he didn't anthropomorphize the animal: the reported animal behavior needed to be true to his animal, the gorilla.

Ben had begun the year as an awkward, reticent writer. His first story about skiing was labored. He worked just to get the events down, to share a little of his personal feelings. Always a hard worker, he stretched in his fiction piece about a kidnapping. He started to take risks: describing more fully, presenting action, and developing a more elaborated story line. The animal paper came next, and with it more risks. In choosing this genre he tried a new way of organizing and presenting information.

11:00 PM NEWS

Welcome to the 11:00 PM news serving gorillas in Rwanda, Zaire and Uganda. I'm Dawn Roberts reporting live from Rwanda, Africa.

Today's top story: a baby, one-year-old, fifteen pound Mountain Gorilla killed viciously by a leopard around noon. The mother Jan Wilde suffered bites on her legs and arms. Dan Williams was at the scene.

"As night falls around this gorilla nest horrified gorilla groups mingle around the area where a leopard jumped out of underbrush on to a baby. The baby was riding on Jan Wilde's back. The mother is in critical condition at a Rwanda hospital. Dan Williams reporting, back to you, Dawn."

Coming up next on the 11:00 gorilla news, Mountain Gorillas get pushed farther up mountains due to humans. Stay with us.

Although it had been presented in another context, Ben remembered the format of the news broadcast and its salient qualities: the cuts, the teasers, and the pacing that our aide had outlined. He incorporated them into his paper. Over the year, Ben's growth as a writer was not marked by sudden leaps, but by steady improvement as he accepted more and more responsibility for all aspects of his writing. Genre initiative was an important step along the way. He could not have done that at the beginning of the year. Then he was preoccupied with creating more elaborated texts. But when we worked on the animal papers, he was ready. He could now own not only what he wanted to say, but how he wanted to say it.

Karin, quiet Karin, spoke through her writing. From the beginning of the year, she was interested in what she could do with the written word. To that end she crafted and recrafted her stories. Always she considered how best to express her intent. She worked hard on her first story about the birth of her brother. Her efforts reflected how much writing mattered to her. But she took greater risks in her animal paper. Following the discussion and examples, Karin asked if she could do her paper not based on a literary genre but on her own experience. While the format is a diary, she turned the beginning into a recapitulation of her own school experience. The information is imparted through a school test, and the studying that she (the chipmunk) did for that test.

May 2, 1975

Dear Diary,

A+
100%
"Yourself" Test
Allstar Elemantary

GRADE: 2nd   DATE: 5/2/75
SEX: Female   AGE: 1 month   DATE OF BIRTH: 4/2/75
NAME: Charlette Chipmunk
HOMEROOM TEACHER: Mrs. Chipette or Mr. Chippyke

1. Describe yourself.

Charlette: I am a girl chipmunk. I am 6 inches long. Grown "mes"
are 10 inches long. I'll be grown-up in 2 months. My tail is NOT
as long as my body, as some animals think. I have beautiful short
silky hair, tinged with a rust here and there, that is mostly gray.
I have black and very light greyish-white stripes on my back in
this order: black, white, black. There's dark brown on the
"outside" of both my black stripes. I am alert and watchful. Light
stripes are across the dark around my eyes. I'm beautiful, lovely,
pretty, etc. !!
Mrs. Chipette: Oh! You sound so modest and pretty, Charlette!

2. What is your favorite season? Your favorite time?

Charlette: My favorite seasons (though I haven't really seen or
heard of two of them) are spring, summer and fall. My favorite
time: late afternoon or early morning. My favorite thing: food.
Mrs. Chipette: Not having ever seen it but knowing that you like
it is called instinct, Charlette. Those seasons are my favorite, too!

3. What would you do if you saw a strange food with a HUMAN
watching you?

Charlette: Run!
Mrs. Chipette: Charlette, you can come up with a better answer!
Let's have it!
Charlette: I'd wait 'til the human left, then I'd circle the food,
running, and then I'd snatch it and run away with it.
Mrs. Chipette: GOOD! I knew you could do it!

4. Who are your enemies?

Charlette: House cats are my worst! Ugh, they're so grotesque.
Then come weasels, "sharp-eyed" hawks, owls (not often),
snakes, foxes, dogs, and HUMANS (not often, either).
Mrs. Chipette: Keep up the good vocabulary, Charlette!

5. Draw a picture of your burrow. Label it.

[Here Karin provided Charlette's illustration.]
Mrs. Chipette: GOOD WORK, CHARLETTE!

6. How do you "communicate" with your friends?

Charlette: I chip-chip on my favorite rock, stump, or log!
Mrs. Chipette: PLEASE try harder to answer more specifically
next time!

7. More about yourself.

Charlette: I weigh 1–5 ounces. I have a bright chestnut rump.
Mrs. Chipette: WONDERFUL! MARVELOUS! SUPERB!

What is so exciting is Karin's use of a nonliterary, though still
written, genre to present the information. I reacted not simply to
the effectiveness of the piece, but also to her inventiveness. Not
only does she have the option of using the explicit and implicit
genres that she reads—the models—she can also use her lived
experience to order and present information. Not bounded by
literary genre, Karin accepts the challenge of creating a new
genre. It is an idea that few of us ever entertain.

Genre Considerations

At a recent poetry reading, Donald Hall discussed a possible
new poetic form that he was working with. Sensing that the
audience shied somewhat at the announcement, he reminded us
that sonnets did not exist until they were invented. Genres are
human inventions. No one had written the short talk piece until
the *New Yorker*'s staff came up with the form. This raises a
number of important issues for me. For several years my school
collected writing samples and scored them holistically. That is,
we graded them on overall impact and did not break the scoring
down into subcategories of organization, mechanics, content,
and style. Discussing the impact of papers in that setting, teachers
acknowledged the importance of genre in their grading response.
The children who took a fresh approach tended to receive
a higher score. A new tack often engages the reader, capturing
one's interest and encouraging attention in a different way. While
acknowledging the importance of newness, I am aware of its

drawbacks. I take Cynthia Ozick's (1983) cautionary note about newness to heart; namely, that what's new is not better per se, that we must guard against overvaluing the new just because it is new. And newness that moves too far beyond the reader's accepted conventions can cause the reader to give up on the text. A prose piece with an implied narrative can violate many of the rules of narrative and still gain acceptance; but it cannot completely ignore the rules of narrative. The assets and liabilities of a fresh approach must be weighed. In my opinion, an example of a work that makes effective use of newness is Italo Calvino's postmodern novel, *If on a Winter's Night a Traveler*. He appears to play fast and loose with narrative but in the end honors enough conventions to sustain the reader's investment in the novel. In fact, all his breaking of the rules must take place within the context of the rules: he expects the reader to know and believe in the conventions of narrative or his book doesn't work. Another good example of a new approach that violates many of the conventions but still stays true to the medium is Woody Allen's *The Purple Rose of Cairo*. The film startles us by having a character break out of the celluloid and move around in the "real" world. That character is also able to take a "real" person into the film world. The premise captures us and then delivers by setting up the tension between the character and the actor who portrays the character. The tension turns the new genre into an asset, forcing the viewer to look differently at the relationship between actor and character.

In the classroom we should foster invention, not simply mimicry; invention not for its own sake, but to create a richer context for the sharing of information and ideas.

The new genres students have tried don't violate the conventions of writing. The novelty is in the fresh way the information is presented. They do engage. The tension comes not in playing off the conventions but in the anthropomorphization of the animal. Something I had seemingly prohibited. The news reporter in Ben's piece talks like hundreds of reporters we've heard. The test in Karin's story is a school test, and the voice in Foxy Loxy is Abby's. These new efforts work because of the tension between the animal and the human dimension. The students are true to the assignment in that the animal behaviors are accurately portrayed. The facts are right, but the format is human, and the juxtaposition produces humor. The children recognize that humor as an important tool for engaging the reader.

Many students are not as actively engaged with information as Brian was in his dolphin story from the animal's perspective. But there must be more than one possible outcome from the assignment, because different learners are at different places in their learning. To expect all the students to be actively working with the information or, alternatively, to think that all of them are ready to take more responsibility for organizing the general framework of a written piece, is to focus too narrowly on the rich interaction between writer and emerging text. Writing can be looked at as solving problems, but we all have different problems and different possible solutions. I must design my assignments to honor the complex nature of learning.

For some of my students, like Brian with his knowledge of dolphin's defenses, the report assignment creates an awareness of ways that writing can put the writer in a different relationship to information. Others discover that they can draw on experiences, literary or nonliterary, to help shape their writing. For still others, the experience of incorporating a number of facts into a lengthy paper may be what they get from the assignment.

As the teacher, I have to be aware of what I demand, expect, invite, and hope for. In this assignment I demand certain things: notes, a hundred facts, a nonstandard report form. I expect the piece to be informative and engaging. To that end I demonstrate what we as a group can agree on as informative and engaging ways to present information. I invite students to take risks in finding powerful ways to express themselves. And I hope that each student will grow as a writer, becoming more aware of the choices implicit in writing, better able to see that certain choices are more efficacious than others, and more aware that to play it safe often diminishes the experience and the work. Six years after "Foxy Loxy" was written, the paper is still fresh in my mind. I have seen and heard the facts many times; what stays with me is the way the facts are presented. Genre is a lens for the writer and the reader, an aid in seeing the material and ourselves.

· 6 ·
Writing Our Way into the Middle Ages

The Middle Ages parades enticingly into our students' lives through movies, computer games, and books. Children are drawn to King Arthur, witches, knights, ladies, castles, jousting, dragons, quests, chivalry. Their imagination is sparked by the period's romance, power, overstated elegance, brutality, and acts of bravery. Wrapped in the myth and mystery of this time, our students welcome the study of the Middle Ages.

Our unit reflects our ideas about learning and knowledge. We do not see social studies as a set of facts and concepts to be simply learned, discussed, and memorized. Rather, social studies, particularly history, is a story to be heard and experienced. We want our students to know the story viscerally, empathetically. As with poetry, they need to get inside the information, so they know it with their emotions as well as their minds. In science it's the difference between talking about experiments and doing them.

In social studies, students feel the weight, restriction, and protection of armor by making suits out of sheet metal. They study, through pictures and text, the properties of the materials that were used and the designs inspired by need and fashion. Then, in pairs, they create and test their own designs, making a helmet, gorget, and breastplate. The pieces must be serviceable in mock combat. Students also design and construct model castles, ones that must be defendable when under direct attack or siege. Using books, pictures, films, and their own imaginations, the students create structures with moats, embrasures, portcullises, and machicolations to guard against siege towers, battering rams, and sappers. The vocabulary of castle architecture becomes a living language of design, not the dead language of memorized fact.

We do the same with the arts of the period. Stained glass windows are made with tissue paper, liquid lead, and plexiglass. While we can't give a strong sense of the developing use of glass in Gothic architecture, we can give students some design experience, making the lead tracery serve like brushstrokes to outline or replicate figures. The students begin to see in stained glass the interplay of line, shape, and color, all brought to life by the infusion of light. Like the armor and the castles, the windows will be used: hung in our Medieval Festival to symbolize a holy space. Making creates the need to learn, and the learning informs and invests the making. Students not only learn about the Middle Ages, but they also begin to think as those in the twelfth or thirteenth century may have thought. Writing, too, helps children enter this time.

A Simulation Game

Seven years ago, after reading Norbert Elias's *Power and Civility* (1939), I decided that I needed to give my students a better, more dynamic understanding of feudalism. We had talked about the relationship between overlord and vassal before, but always in static terms, defining the role of each but not setting the interplay in motion. Elias's book is important precisely because he emphasizes the richness of that interplay. Briefly, Elias argues that a feudal lord was much like a modern American corporation. As such, the feudal lord could not stand still; either he had to be growing—by conquest, treaty, or alliance—or he was seen as a prime target for takeover. The feudal lord's active acquisition of lands and allegiances created a number of awkward and intricate relationships. A lord might owe allegiance to opposing sides in a major conflict. In such a situation the lord might openly pledge homage to each of the overlords, while secretly claiming more support to one. Gies, in *Life in a Medieval Castle* (1974), quotes one such set of relationships, this from the fifteenth century:

> If it should happen that the Count of Grandpre should be at war with the Countess and Count of Champagne for his own personal grievances, I will personally go to the assistance of the Count of Grandpre and will send to the Countess and Count of Champagne, if they summon me, the knights I owe for the fief which I hold of them. But if the Count of Grandpre shall make war on the Countess and Count of Champagne on behalf of his friends and not for his own personal grievances, I shall serve in person with the Countess and Count of Champagne and I will send one knight to the Count of Grandpre. (p. 53)

I wanted my students to have a sense of interrelationships. I decided that I could best give them this sense through a simulation. I began with some trepidation, however, because I am not personally comfortable with role playing.

The goal of our simulation game is to gain control of an imaginary country. The king or queen controls the country at the beginning and can win simply by remaining in control at the end. The others can win if they unseat the monarch. But to do so they have to form a number of alliances. Only in groups can they attack other vassals, and only in larger alliances can they attempt to attack the king or queen. They begin the game owing allegiance to certain overlords and can break those allegiances only through warfare. To form alliances many of the lords have the additional trump card of children, who can be married off in return for privileges or favors. The game, then, forces students to experience the dynamic relationships of feudalism, as they work within a structure of commitments and countercommitments to maximize individual and collective power.

We all know how game players can subvert a game's intentions. Basically, game players want to find out how to win; they worry much less about the persona they are supposed to adopt. So my students became immediately interested and knowledgeable about the point value of different throws of the die. This was one of my concerns with simulations: that the simulation may get lost in the preoccupation with playing and winning. My solution to this problem was to introduce and require game journals to be kept by each participant. After each move, the player has to translate his or her move and reaction into a historical description. The entry is a single draft. I am not looking for polished writing, just reflection: a way of recasting the move into the appropriate context. Here is a journal entry by Karin that strongly mirrors the preceding fifteenth century account:

> Boohoo. Talk about bad luck. So many things have happened in the past four months I could just die. First of all, I'm considering going against Lord Alison (an ally). She has "borrowed" as she calls it, ll of my men to lend to Lord Hjalti (he's inconsiderate when it comes to plans, he should be a peasant) so that he can attack Queen Sara. She is having such a hard time. She is under two sieges (one by Sir Jack, the other by "Lord" Hjalti) and is still trying to find some way to reward my loyalty. "Lord" Hjalti is such a rat! Speaking of rats, Sir Joey decided to attack me. I tried to protest, but I had to stop because he was about to trample one of my best men, Edward, with a battering ram! Well, at least I saved Edward, but not my castle. It's a wreck! We have been trying to repair the door for weeks, but at least we can get in and out of the castle. The peasants rebelled last week, and all the lords lost more than five men each. So did poor Queen Sara! They lay it all on her. Oh, I forgot to tell you, Joey took nine of my men. One of them was Edward. I learned another horrible thing—fair Lord Lynn turned against Queen Sara! They used to call us the Talkative Three, we were so together and loud. Oh well. I have a question for you journal—Why is bad luck following me around? See if you can answer it next time. Good-bye!
>
> Sincerely yours,
> Distressed Karin

This entry epitomizes Karin's state of emotional and strategic flux in the game. She owes Lord Alison eleven knights' service as part of her fealty. Lord Alison, in turn, lends them to Lord Hjalti to be used against Karin's own friend, Queen Sara. This causes Karin to reconsider her allegiance to her own overlord. At the same time she learns that her friend Lord Lynn has also turned against Queen Sara. Karin does not seem prepared to turn against the Queen herself, in part because Queen Sara still intends to reward her for past loyalties. Later on in the game Queen Sara does make Karin a lord, but this leads to Karin's downfall, as several lords, including former compatriots, band together to attack her for supporting the Queen. Like the fifteenth-century example, Karin finds herself and her men on both sides of several situations. She, as they, must struggle to do what is right and in one's own best interests. The three throws of the die force her to give men to Lord Alison, to fight and lose to Joey, and to become aware that Lord Lynn will attack Queen Sara. Through her journal entry those moves are placed into the context of competing loyalties. Granted, some of the language and imagery is forced. Having Edward almost run over by a battering ram doesn't really work. Nor does the "boohoo" opening. But in this one-draft entry Karin has captured what we know of the relationships. And it is the writing that assures me the effort is being made; connections are being felt. Karin's last entry continues her theme of ill-luck. Even though she has been made lord, bad weather confirms her fatalistic feelings. It seems likely that these feelings enshrouded many in this time of competing loyalties, played out in constant maneuvering and warfare.

April 20, 1490

Journal (may God save your soul), when will I *ever* win a fight with Lady Amy? As usual, I ruined my weapon, the battering ram this time, and I lost 4 men. Now that I'm a lord, the other lords seem to be shaken up because I'm a new lord and seemed to have gone against me. It's raining bad luck and water, and even the sun's bright rays don't help to bring good luck, even though they arouse my spirits. Well, farewell 'till next time.

Sincerely yours,
Miserable Karin

Note:
It has been found out that Lady Karin had been attacked by the other lords. In extreme poverty, she died. Her children, Thomas, John, Charlie, Isabel and Tara were soon raised to the position of lords by Queen Sara. When Queen Sara died, her last words were written upon a big scroll. They were: "Make Thomas Velez King of Alacasonne." These orders were carried out, and immediately

the other lords (except for his sisters and brothers) went against him. They tried to attack him but he killed them all. The other 4 children became the 4 main lords. "Victory for the Velez's!" is what has been said for many years. The history of the Velez family brings me back the memory of Lady Karin Velez stating to her journal the phrase, "The castle no one could attack without losing, the one that belonged to Sir Velez and his family . . ." so clear that I can almost picture the family gathered around the picture in the church—bold and brave, pretty and handsome, loving and gentle.

The simulation was a new teaching tool for me. I had used journals before, but not over such an extended period of time, and not to translate an experience. For too long I had limited social studies writing to responding to questions: to measure knowledge or force synthesis. Such use of writing reduced student work to list making. Even open-ended questions called for an academic response. Certainly there is validity to writing this way. Lists can be a powerful way of coming to know. But leaving written work at that can forfeit deepening understanding. Much of the formal writing (answering such questions or instructions as "What are three causes for the rise of monasticism?" or "Describe feudalism") keeps students on the outside of the information. The journal invites them to get inside, to imagine themselves as lord , bishop, or knight. Our festivals call on them to act out the part.

Festivals and Productions

All schools develop traditions. Our school has a tradition of holding festivals to culminate and celebrate learning, particularly in social studies. We've had Japanese, Mexican, Greek, Native American, Colonial, and New Hampshire festivals. Typically, the festivals integrate subject areas and are experiential in nature. Music, movement, visual arts, and language arts are all part of every festival. In many, we also find ways to include science and math. When we began the medieval unit nine years ago, culminating the unit with a festival was a foregone conclusion. At first the festival included a fashion show in ersatz medieval garb (with heavy reliance on bathrobes), medieval delicacies like cucumber in cinnamon, and games like roll the hoop or stilt walking. The festival provided children a chance to tilt at quintains like a squire would, make and launch paper boats carrying a candle and a wish from one side of a water table to the other, do model brass rubbings, and sing "Sumer is a cumen in." There was plenty of activity, and learning took place for the fifth grade presenters and for the audience.

Beginning to teach the medieval unit coincided with my personal involvement in amateur theatrical productions. Called Revels, the productions combine music, dance, drama, and ritual. They portray traditions of various cultures. and connect those cultures with our own. Revels loosely tells a story, trying to stay true to the traditions and music, believing that there is more power in those traditions then in a tightly crafted story. My direct involvement has been minimal; I have struggled to hide my lack of musicianship in sword and Morris dance teams. But the experience has had a profound effect on my teaching, and particularly on the school's Medieval Festival. With this personal involvement, I began to look for ways to make our school festival richer and more faithful to the original material.

In our school library I found a copy of medieval miracle plays rewritten for children. I had some students make further adaptations of these plays, and we then incorporated them into our festivities. At the same time, we ordered a copy of Madeleine Cosman's book, *Medieval Holidays and Festivals* (1981). Her book includes a shortened version of a medieval mummer's play. Mummer's plays have a distinctive style. The play is less a play and more a set of character speeches directed at the audience. Typically a number of characters introduce themselves; an evil force (dragon or Turk) assaults a princess; St. George comes to the rescue and then dies a ritual death, executed by a sword team. He is brought back to life by a fool who uses the powers of nature. There is a minimal amount of stage interaction. The play relies on rhyme, humor, and topicality. Much of this perfectly matches fifth-grade theatrical sensibilities. Many ten-year-olds have difficulty remaining in character on stage, but many students love to act. This seemed a perfect vehicle.

I gave some students the opportunity to read Cosman's version of the play and then to write their own adaptation. They had to stay true to the basic plot sequence, while trying to make their version engaging. Some tried topicality; one was a Sweet Valley High version ("I mean like that dragon is totally grody to the max, but . . ." or "That is a genuine preppy prince and Bunny is his nickname"). Even in versions that remained truer to the medieval time, students have experimented with wording and ideas. For example, here are the opening lines in Cosman's model of a mummer's play for summer:

> KING: Woe is me, my darling daughter,
>   That I must live and see your slaughter.

And here are four different sets of opening lines to four mummer's plays written by fifth graders:

> KING (*sobbing*): Oh my what shall I do my two Valley Girl
>   daughters are going to be eaten by Dodo the dragon.

> KING: Rue this day, I, the kind king say,
>   From now on this kingdom will have no holiday.
>   Alas, I give my daughter away,
>   For that fierce dragon to slay!
>   Oh, daughter, as you stand so sweet,
>   With bridal gown down to your feet,
>   I give you a blessing as here you await,
>   The bad dragon's eating and your terrible fate.

> KIND KING: I'm sorry, dear daughter but the dragon's on the
>   loose, He's eaten every animal, including the moose.
>   One hundred brave young knights have died at his will,
>   Though I've offered him riches, you're the dragon's next kill.
>   Even though it breaks my heart I cannot tell a lie,
>   The dragon wants you, and you're going to have to die.

> ST. GEORGE: Rue this day
>   For I, St. George, will
>   Say I'll kill
>   The dragon dead away.
>   My cottage is ruined
>   My parents are dead
>   My sisters and brothers have already fled.

The writers of these four beginnings have paid attention to the example, but are not bound by it. The basic information in each is the same: the dragon is terrorizing the neighborhood and must be appeased. The specific form and tone varies with each play. The students find ways within the general format to assert their individuality ("St. George will use his sword and cross/And if you wish, his dental floss"). The fourth beginning doesn't even start with the King, but with St. George. Yet that student also stayed true to the sense of the play, offering the daughter to the dragon.

In this work the students have an experience analogous to the medieval storyteller. They receive the story—in this case in both written and oral form because they have attended the plays of the previous four years—and reproduce the play while making it their own. Obviously they are not as steeped in the tradition, and therefore not bound by the material in the same way. But after experiencing the material for four years as an audience member, they do have a sense of responsibility in re-presenting the story. Like the game "Operator," they are bound in what they say by what they have heard. Their play incorporates both the tradition and their own sensibilities.

I found myself in the same position, trying to present traditional material in my own words. I was asked to help write a skit about a medieval church feast, "The Feast of Fools," for a Christmas Revels. In this feast, the church hierarchy is turned upside down. A boy is named bishop; the service itself is often brayed instead of sung; and clerics can hurl insults at their superiors. Working on the script proved a daunting experience. Even though I had asked students to write plays, I had given little thought to the difficulties of writing dialogue. As I started to write, I realized that few of the words did the work I wanted them to. I worked on the script with two fellow revelers. We wrote and talked, rewrote and talked, all the while trying to imagine the effect of our words in play form. For instance, we felt that we had to introduce the skit by giving the audience some sense of what the Feast of Fools was about, but we wanted to do it in keeping with the rest of the skit. We came up with the following:

BOY BISHOP: The year has come round and none too soon
    For lords and church to grant this boon:
    The occasion . . . The Feast of Fools,
    Where none are governed by any rules.
    The low are exalted,
    The mighty defaulted,
    Reason's unseated,
    The cellar's depleted,
    Ceremony's stood on its head!
    Why, we get up . . . by going to bed!

In those few short lines we hoped to convey the meaning, sense, and rhythm of what was to follow. At best, I was only partially successful. There were problems with the words. "Defaulted" doesn't exactly work. It's too strong a word, too formal next to "mighty," and the meaning isn't what we were after: lords didn't default as much as accept a temporary displacement. And the last line, the one about getting up, pulls the listener away from the action. We kept the line because it offered a clear sense of inversion, but the example had nothing to do with the action on stage. Just as important, the lines went by too quickly; many audience members never did get the sense of what they were watching. Written text has a different pace than spoken text, and we didn't adequately understand that in writing our script. I point all this out to suggest ways students learn as they write their adaptations of the mummer's play. The plays are presented and the students get audience feedback, both immediate response to the performance through laughter and applause, and long-term in comments after the production about what other children and adults understood and could follow. From writing their mummer's plays students can learn a great deal about medieval folk beliefs. They have the experience of playing directly to an audience, of exploring the effect of words and pacing, of confronting the difficulties of turning a written piece into a spoken production.

After having students write mummer's plays and miracle plays, and especially after writing my own skit, I became convinced of two things: I wanted to make our festival more dramatic production than experiential crafts show; and using writing to create short skits or pieces was more appropriate than having students draft a thirty- or forty-minute play. Having reached those conclusions, I came up with two solutions in subsequent years. First, I wrote three short skits myself, one about town life, another about castle life, and a third about warfare. Within each I created spaces or opportunities for students to create pieces like the mummer's play, based on existing genres—poems, riddles, stories. Several years ago I altered this arrangement, combining the skits to create an overarching play, *The Last Days of Henry II.*

The main forum for student-written pieces is the banquet scene. Richard The Lionhearted and Eleanor of Aquitaine entertain Philip, King of France. True to what we know about medieval entertainment, the royal party sees and hears bards, storytellers, troubadours, jugglers, even a trained bear act.

The storytellers get their sense of medieval story in part from a prose translation of *Beowulf* by Robert Nye (1968). The whole fifth grade reads the story. The first year I resisted having all the students read it because I thought it was beyond some of them. It isn't. *Beowulf* deals precisely with those ideas that fascinate ten-year-olds: the fight between good and evil, the faces of human courage, and the acceptance of limitations. Students made clear that first year that they wanted in on a good story, so now we all read it. And as we read it we discuss ways to portray evil, ways to represent the fight between good and evil, and why Beowulf must face more than one evil force. We try our hand at drawing evil; what does pure evil look like? Then several students write a description of an encounter between good and evil, and we use them in our banquet scene.

Here is Aaron's story. As you read it keep in mind the way he portrays good and evil, how much power each has, and the way that the outcome is decided.

Here's a story to tell about Sir Edward's and Sir Thomas's brave battle with the dragon.

"Ahhh. You won, I give up." said Sir Thomas.

"Good, I won again. Would you like to rematch later?" asked Sir Edward.

"Sure, why not." said Sir Thomas.

"You know the King's offered five hundred pounds if you can kill the dragon, and to prove it you have to bring him the dragon's 5 golden fangs. I'm going to try it," said Sir Edward.

"I'll do it too," said Sir Thomas.

"Good, I'll meet you at dawn, here. I'll have the blacksmith fix us the best armour he can find," said Sir Edward.

"I'll be ready at dawn," said Sir Thomas.

[*Dawn*]

"Sir Edward do you have my armour?" asked Sir Thomas.

"Indeed I do, it's at my manor house. We have to work here though, because we don't want anybody to know about our plan," said Sir Edward. "What I was thinking we could do is . . ."

[*At Sun Rise*]

"Sir Thomas are you almost ready?" asked Sir Edward.

"Yes, just let me get my helmet."

[*At the Cave*]

"Do you remember the plan?" asked Sir Edward.

"Yes I do," said Sir Thomas.

Sir Edward climbed on top of the end of the cave. While Sir Thomas found his way to the dragon's den. He gathers up all his courage and he threw a stone at the dragon, and hit him. The dragon jumped up ready for battle, but saw nothing because Sir Thomas jumped behind a rock. The dragon turned around to see if there was anybody behind him. Of course there wasn't. Sir Thomas jumped out from behind the rock and yelled, "Yo dragon, over here."

The dragon turned around, and blew a big gust of wind, knocking Sir Thomas back. He ran with all his might towards the end of the cave, where Sir Edward was waiting with a crossbow. Sir Thomas rushed out of the cave.

"Get ready, get ready . . . NOW!"

Sir Edward fired an arrow straight at the dragon's forehead. It knocked off a scale. He fired another right into the dragon's head. The dragon roared out in pain. Sir Thomas took his sword and cut off the dragon's toenails, making sure he couldn't use them anymore. The dragon took one claw and swiped at Sir Thomas. Sir Thomas put up his shield, but it didn't help at all, because the dragon's razor sharp claws went straight through his shield and also his armour. Sir Thomas cried out in agonizing pain. Then, the dragon took the other claw and swiped at Sir Edward missing by hairs. While the dragon was distracted, Sir Thomas took a rope and tied the dragon's legs together, then pulled. The dragon fell to the ground. Sir Edward took his dagger and he threw the first one straight at the roots of one of the dragon's teeth. It fell out and as that happened, one of the dragon's arms turned to stone.

"Incredible," said Sir Edward.

Now that the dragon's feet and one arm were not useful all they needed to do was turn the other arm to stone. Sir Edward threw his second dagger and missed. He finally took out his third dagger and threw it. It knocked out the furthest back tooth and the dragon's whole body turned to stone, accept for his three remaining teeth. They fell to the ground. Sir Edward helped Sir Thomas bandage up his leg. Then they collected the five golden teeth and rode home and got the money.

Back at the Manor house Sir Edward and Sir Thomas were telling about the battle:

"His eyes were redder than hell itself, and his claws sharper than the sharpest razor. His breath was the worst thing about him. The first time I smelled it I was about to faint, and his body had the reddest scales you've ever seen. But me and Sir Thomas can do anything . . ."

In addition to the storytellers, we have several bards, who speak the praises of the assembled dignitaries. As a model, I read the medieval poem "The death of King Edward I" from *Medieval English Lyrics* (Davies 1964). The poem reads in part:

> Alle that beth of herte trewe
> A stounde herkneth to my song:
> Of del that Deth hath dight us newe,
> That maketh me sike and sorewe among;
> Of a knight that wes so strong,
> Of wham God hath don his wille.
> Me thuncheth that Deth hath don us wrong
> That he so sone shall ligge stille.

We discuss the tone of the poem, the kind of information conveyed, and the position of the poet in relation to the subject, the king. Then several students draft and revise poems to be spoken during the banquet. Here are two poems to suggest the range of writing. The first maintains a consistent tone; the second is inconsistent in tone, but for the most part addresses the subject appropriately.

KING RICHARD
My kind Sir Richard is said to be cruel
Many servants hated his law and despotic rule.
But really my lord is very kind.
This of course you will find,
But as you might have guessed
His kindness will not everyone bless.
Anyone evil must fall to the ground
For everyone by justice must be bound.
Many a day Richard's gone joy riding
Hunting fox or with other knights colliding
But one fine day he trotted down the lane
A shadow formed, one that suggested pain.
But my lord kept on trotting
All the while in the distance an evil shadow plotting.
My lord now before the dragon stood
Aware this beast had not one ounce of good.
All six heads stared at this noble knight
Each head a hideous evil sight.
Out of one a great eye flickered a dancing flame.
The second made an even greater claim
Between teeth and tongue shot a fire bright
Threatening body and soul of this noble knight
But my Richard did not run, nor even shake
Instead he drew his sword, the dragon's life to take.
He focused on the fire-breathing head
And charged, only to be knocked back, his face blood red.
The fight went on with Richard losing,
This of course was not of his choosing.
It looked as if the dragon had defeated
As he bent down for the final beating,
Richard with his last ounce of strength
Thrust his sword through the dragon's length.

A moment of silence, the dragon stood still
Then fell to the ground, Richard's latest kill.
Once again Richard had proven true to his creed:
Evil must be smitten by courageous deed.

LORD RICHARD
My Lord Richard is very mighty
Though he never keeps his castle tidy.

He's slayed many dragons with one powerful blow
But never once stooped to fight mean and low.

He fought the fearless sea
But is always kind to me.

He's fought many battles, always won
And never once thought to run.

But the most courageous time of all
Was the time he made the giant fall.

Ten feet tall, with scales galore was the giant
He killed deer in the forest with one squeeze
And never once used the word please
He had a quick temper and was always defiant.

The giant met Richard at dawn
To see who had more brawn.

They would fight till one was dead
No matter how much both bled.

The giant was mistaken
He thought Milord Richard could be easily taken.

They fought all day and into the night
Ripping up trees both left and right

Tired and wounded they both fought on
Till their strength was nearly gone.

Finally Sir Richard caught him by surprise
And hit him a mighty blow between the eyes.

With the crushing blow
The blood began to flow.

In another instant the giant was still
Ready to be buried under a nearby hill.

So I give you Sir Richard, brave and strong.
May his strength increase and his life be long.

Here the students are using poetry in a way different from that discussed in chapter three, but consistent with the use made of poetry in the Middle Ages. They get a sense that poetry can be, and was, used to praise through narrative description with personal interjections. Students can contrast that use of poetry with modern poetry not only with regard to form or content, but also with regard to a sense of self. What did it mean for the common person that formal language was used almost exclusively to describe the deeds and attributes of the nobility, or that it dealt little with inner thoughts or feelings? This is a question we only approach tangentially, but one that we can get a better sense of through "walking" inside the literature of the period than through an abstract discussion of feudalism.

In our banquet scene we also play with language as medieval people did: in riddles. There are a number of Anglo-Saxon riddles. Here is one:

Our world is lovely in different ways,
Hung with beauty and works of the hands.
I saw a strange machine, made
For motion, slide against the sand,
Shrieking as it went. It walked swiftly
On its only foot, this odd shaped monster,
Travelled in an open country without
Seeing, without arms, without hands,
With many ribs, and its mouth in the middle.
Its work is useful, and welcome, for it leads
Its belly with food, and brings abundance

To men, to poor and to rich, paying
Its tribute year after year. Solve
This riddle if you can, and unravel its name.
Answer: A Boat

The following pieces show how Martin interacted with the
examples, internalizing the tone of the original, while making
the genre his own.

The impact shatters me,
And makes me whine,
But I bear it and come to give dread to my foe.
I go at great speed.
Enemies dread me,
But I can't blame them
Well here I go
To battle in great glory
The king yells for me to attack, to his peasants
I go and soon make a gash in an enemy's body.
What may I ask is my name?
Answer: A Sword

I stand very tall and guard thy lord and all ye subjects
Through rain and snow
I help my lord.
People gaze in awe at my awesome strength
As they yield.
Men come and defeat the on-coming attackers.
They go slashing and crashing at the enemy near.
Men die and thy king orders more men.
I was born from the ground and partly from man.
I serve man well.
I was then cut with sharp tools and made very well.
My lord is proud of the work that the serfs did
And I am proud of pleasing my lord.
What is my name?
Answer: A Castle

In these two examples Martin's writing voice changes. All his
other writing had been direct, with little development or embel-
lishment. Here he takes in the Anglo-Saxon model and uses it to

help generate his own riddles. Martin's riddles are stylized. He uses archaic language and the circuitous presentation of information. Much of his analysis of the model occurred internally. I am sure that he could not verbalize all the components of an Anglo-Saxon riddle that he tries to incorporate in his own. This is an example of learning empathetically, not by definition but by experience, as Martin receives and then produces the genre.

Writing can be used in a number of ways to help bring about understanding in social studies. There are times when direct question-and-answer is the best written assignment. When we want to know if a student knows 8 × 6 we don't want an elaborated story to display the knowledge. The same is true when assessing whether or not a student has a basic understanding of the role of tournaments in the Middle Ages; he or she doesn't have to draft a play to present the knowledge. Often, however, we ask for the knowledge in this form too soon, believing that asking and answering questions, demanding conciseness immediately, will produce informed knowledge. I doubt it. I can give a definition of photosynthesis that might pass muster, but it is not well informed. I don't really have a picture of chloroplasts, nor have I played with cells enough to know what I'm talking about. That is the problem with much of social studies. Reading and writing that is limited to factual information doesn't let the learner get inside the information. Reading viewed as modeling and writing to recreate the genres of the period give students the opportunity to play with sensibilities from another time, to start to sense how others thought and felt.

The production worked better than the fair. Even though students were instructing others in the fair, they were kept on the outside of the information. As instructors they did not become medieval characters. They dispensed information rather than living it vicariously. The production required writer, actor, dancer, and singer to draft and redraft the information, to get inside it.

Four years ago I was cast in the Christmas Revels' mummer's play as the fool. Over the weeks of rehearsal I struggled, as my students struggle, to come to terms with my character. As I did so I began to sense what I imagine a medieval man did as he went from house to house presenting a play that made some sense to him, but not complete sense; that called him back to an earlier time not completely understood; that permitted frivolity while pointing to the mysteries of the earth. In creating that character, I experienced what I want for my students.

Several years ago a parent came to me after our production. She said that she had enjoyed the show but had had some misgivings about all the time spent in rehearsal, working on songs, dialogue, and dances. Those misgivings, however, were allayed when she heard her son explaining to a younger sibling the meaning and significance of the tournament for medieval knights. Understanding can grow so much more richly from living in and with the material. I don't see myself creating poets, novelists, or poor copyists of other traditions; rather, I see myself helping students to learn and, most important, to learn how to learn. I've come to theater and writing late in life, in part because of my temperament, but also because of the way I was educated. I have some sense now of what those forms have to offer a learner, and I want my students to know that too—empathetically, of course.

EPILOGUE

■

Learning never ends. I am constantly learning new things about myself and the world. That does not mean I always want to learn new things or that I always understand what I am learning. But my classroom work and my teaching at UNH have enabled me to be more open to experiences and to let those experiences inform my teaching practices and beliefs. A recent trip to Germany helped clarify my understanding of writing-process teaching.

I couldn't believe my luck: I was invited to work with American teachers in Germany. Afterward, I would have five days to travel on my own. Throughout the trip, I would have the chance to reacquaint myself with German, a language I hadn't used in twenty years. My plan for the last five days was to visit two beautiful medieval walled cities, Dinkelsbuhl and Rothenberg; to visit two cathedral cities, Bamberg and Regensberg; and to spend time in Munich. I made a pact with myself to use German, and only German, when traveling alone.

I didn't keep the pact the first week. When opportunities presented themselves, I reverted to using English or simply didn't speak. The second day there, my car was towed from its parking place. I met with the police to find the car's whereabouts. I spoke only English despite the fact that their understanding of the language was limited. I felt myself retreating into my natural shyness, a shyness compounded by my not having been a good student of German. That whole first week I spoke no German except to order meals.

After the last class on Friday I went to get my car rental. Again I was all too willing to let the station manager practice his high school English. I was not ready to risk speaking German myself.

The car rented, I left Erding Saturday morning for Dinkelsbuhl. Cocooned within the car, I turned on a German radio station and recognized—nothing. Only when the announcer spoke of "Gewitter" did I recognize a word. (Actually, I misrecognized the word for thunderstorm, thinking it meant weather. But I was close.) The announcer continued, talking about the news, I guessed. Instrumental music provided relief; then I could stop trying to figure out sounds, stop realizing how little German I knew. For four hours I drove, stopping only once for food— ordered by pointing—and gas. By the time I arrived in Dinkelsbuhl I better understood the weather report: "Bedeckt mit Gewitter und heiss." Seeing the clouds and hearing the thunder helped.

Like the butterfly, my cocooned existence had to end. But I felt no transformation. I wasn't ready to "fly" in German. To know a few weather words wasn't enough. Yet fly I must. I parked outside the town and walked down the hill. Where were the walls? I could see several low structures; were they the walls? Passing through a gate, the town lay before me: an impressionistic painting with tall stucco houses in pastel colors, each one a different shade of green, yellow, and gray, with an occasional pink thrown in. And everywhere, houses were dotted with flower boxes exuding pure color, red or white.

With a town map I walked the streets, taking in the rococo architecture but wanting more of a sense of enclosed space— walls. Walking in another direction I came to a partial gate, but no real wall. A crowd had formed outside the gate, waiting to listen to an American rock group. Doubly disappointed, I got back in the car and headed for Rothenberg. I hadn't spoken a word.

I came upon Rothenberg before I realized it. I was in the country, stopped at a traffic light, and there on the left was a wall

connected to a gate. Walking briskly I encountered the foregate
sentried by two turreted towers. Then came an inner gate with a
high main tower. Stairs to the left led to a wall walk. Now that
I was there, I postponed walking it, choosing instead to first see
the town from below. I walked its radius and then its circumfer-
ence. But I could not continue to postpone the pleasure of the
wall walk. Upon reaching the central square, I headed toward the
open stairway. Both the steps and the wall walk were so narrow
that all were forced to move single file. From my vantage point
on the north side, I could see that three-quarters of the town was
defined by the wall. The wall was clearly marked by the brick red
tiled roof, supported by rough-hewn timbers. It varied in height
from ten to twenty-five feet and was in excellent condition, having been repaired over the last ten years. Names and dates etched
in marble stones in the wall acknowledged the financial support
for the rebuilding. From this vantage point I could see that not all
of the town was main streets laden with tourist shops. Hungry
and needing a place to sleep, I left the wall and began walking the
side streets. Around a corner I encountered my favorite kind of
shop: a bargain bookstore. Not only a bargain bookstore, but one
that specialized in things medieval: facsimile manuscripts, calli-
graphic paper, and illuminated manuscript pages. I couldn't
resist. In the doorway I picked up a copy of the Heidelberg
manuscript, leafed through it, loved it, but put it back because it
was 58 DM, or $29. I looked for the individual manuscript pages,
couldn't find them, and had to decide whether to surrender to my
hunger or get help from the salesperson. How does one ask?
What's the word for "illuminated" or even "page," for that matter? It seemed too much trouble, but I was interested. I
approached the woman, the question still forming in my mind.
"Haben sie noch das Blatim Fenster?"
  "Können sie einen Moment warten? Dann kann ich Ihnen
zeigen."
  The flood of words I had triggered engulfed me. I managed
"Ja." I felt exhilarated. I had been understood even if I didn't
understand her reply. After being shown the papers and choosing
one, I ventured another question about food: "Können sie mir
empfehlen irgendwo zum essen?" She replied "Ja" and proceeded
to direct me to an inexpensive Gasthaus. With that my German

experience began. For the next five days, by choice, I spoke, heard, lived only German. I made many mistakes, only partially understood conversations and directions, butchered German case endings, but got to do what I wanted to: visited the cathedrals, ate well, tracked down Kathe Kruse dolls for my daughters, and found an excellent set of recorders.

In those five days as I walked and talked, I met specters from my past: Frau Donovan, my high school German teacher, glaring at me as I mispronounced *zwölf* or forgot the gender of *Hund*; my college German teachers—teaching assistants really—gloating as I misremembered memorized dialogue, only too willing to point out my mistakes. Those experiences had led me to silence.

Now I would speak. Why? Being in Germany was not reason enough. I had been in Germany for several days and had availed myself of English whenever I could. No, the change was more deep-seated than just being in a certain locale. Walking the streets of Munich I realized that the desire to speak in German came from a desire to be heard, and that this desire was fostered by my writing, more accurately by my writing experience.

The writing-process experience—writing, sharing, responding—has taught me, convinced me at last, that being right isn't most important. Communicating is. We don't speak to be right but to make contact, to explore, to play, to figure out, to understand.

In one antique shop I spent an hour discussing the growing disparity between rich and poor with the shop owner, an older German who had just returned from a visit to Los Angeles and Las Vegas. We spoke not to be right, but to match our human outrage across cultures. He simplified his language to meet me. I reached for language to meet him. We didn't simplify our concern or ideas but instead augmented language with gesture. As the conversation drew to a close he applauded my German. Inaccurate or generous though his assessment was, I felt good. We had talked.

We had talked, and I have written to tear down walls. Walled cities offer an exciting glimpse into the past, but they aren't the present or the future. Neither is walled learning: separating self from self, shrouded in the desire for correctness; or separating information from learning, facts from their use. The point of learning is to come to know, not to already know. And learning is experienced in community. The writing process has helped me dismantle the wall of correctness, not only in writing, but in all areas of learning. I seek to replace the wall with a more open field in which my mind can embrace ideas and people. Fear of failure is not completely erased, but eased.

Now, thinking of German, I see not only Frau Donovan's face but also that of the antique dealer. I hear not only her correction, but also his praise. As a result of that kind of encouragement, I will continue to speak, write, and learn.

BIBLIOGRAPHY

■

Alexander, Lloyd. 1964. *The Book of Three*. New York: Holt, Rinehart & Winston.

Beowulf. 1968. *A new telling by Robert Nye*. New York: Bantam Doubleday Dell.

Burnett, Frances. 1962. *The Secret Garden*. Philadelphia: Lippincott.

Calkins, Lucy. 1986. *The Art of Teaching Writing*. Portsmouth, NH: Heinemann.

Calvino, Italo. 1981. *If on a Winter's Night a Traveler*. New York: Harcourt Brace Jovanovich.

Cosman, Madeleine. 1981. *Medieval Holidays and Festivals: A Calendar of Celebrations*. New York: Scribner's.

Dahl, Roald. 1984. *Boy*. New York: Farrar, Straus, & Giroux.

Davies, R. T., ed. 1964. *Medieval English Lyrics*. Chicago: Northwestern University Press.

Dillard, Annie. 1987. *An American Childhood*. New York: Harper & Row.

DuBois, William Pene. 1965. *The Alligator Case*. New York: Harper & Row.

———. 1966. *The Three Policemen*. New York: Viking.

———. 1967. *The Horse in the Camel Suit*. New York: Harper & Row.

Dunning, Stephen, Edward Lueders, and Hugh Smith, comp. 1966. *Reflections on the Gift of a Watermelon Pickle*. New York: Lothrop, Lee & Shepard.

Eckert, Allan W. 1971. *Incident at Hawk's Hill*. Boston: Little, Brown.

Elias, Norbert. 1939. *Power and Civility*. New York: Pantheon.

Gardner, Martin. 1961. *The Second Scientific American Book of Math Puzzles and Diversions*. New York: Simon & Schuster.

George, Jean Craighead. 1978. *The Wounded Wolf*. New York: Harper & Row.

Gies, Joseph and Francis. 1974. *Life in a Medieval Castle*. New York: Harper & Row.

Grahame, Kenneth. 1960. *Wind in the Willows*. New York: Scribner's.

Graves, Donald. 1983. *Writing: Teachers and Children at Work*. Portsmouth, NH: Heinemann.

Hall, Donald. 1988. *Poetry and Ambition*. Ann Arbor: University of Michigan Press.

Jarrall, Randall. 1967. "A Bat is Born." In Bill Martin Jr., *Sounds of Mystery*. New York: Holt, Rinehart & Winston.

Juster, Norton. 1961. *The Phantom Tollbooth*. New York: Random House.

Kipling, Rudyard. 1907. *Just So Stories*. Garden City, New York: Doubleday.

Larkin, Philip. 1964. *The Whitsun Weddings*. New York: Random House.

Livingston, Myra Cohn. 1984. *Child as Poet: Myth or Reality?* Boston: Horn Book.

Moffett, James. 1968. *A Student-Centered Language Arts Curriculum, Grades K–6: A Handbook for Teachers*. Boston: Houghton Mifflin.

————. 1992. *Student-Centered Language Arts, K–12*. Portsmouth, NH: Boynton/Cook-Heinemann.

Nolan, Christopher. 1987. *Under the Eye of the Clock*. New York: St. Martin's Press, Inc.

O'Neill, Mary. 1961. *Hailstones and Halibut Bones*. Garden City, NY: Doubleday.

Ozick, Cynthia. 1983. *Art and Ardor*. New York: Knopf.

Paterson, Katherine. 1977. *Bridge to Terabithia*. New York: Crowell.

————. 1978. *The Great Gilly Hopkins*. New York: Crowell.

Piaget, Jean. 1952. *The Child's Concept of Number*. London: Routledge & Kegan Paul.

Rosenthal, H. L. 1987. *The Poet's Art*. New York: Norton.

Shahn, Ben. 1957. The Shaping of Content. Cambridge: Harvard University Press.

Taylor, Theodore. 1969. *The Cay*. New York: Avon Books.

Turgenev, Ivan. 1967. "The Quail." In Bill Martin Jr., *Sounds of a Distant Drum*. New York: Holt, Rinehart & Winston.